English for Mass Communication

— 2023 Edition —

Hirofumi Horie
Kaori Kato
Kazuhisa Konishi
Shuji Miyazaki
Yasuko Uchino

ASAHI PRESS

音声再生アプリ「リスニング・トレーナー」を使った音声ダウンロード

朝日出版社開発のアプリ、「リスニング・トレーナー（リストレ）」を使えば、教科書の音声をスマホ、タブレットに簡単にダウンロードできます。どうぞご活用ください。

◉ アプリ【リスニング・トレーナー】の使い方

《アプリのダウンロード》

App Store または Google Play から「リスニング・トレーナー」のアプリ（無料）をダウンロード

App Storeはこちら▶

Google Playはこちら▶

《アプリの使い方》

① アプリを開き「コンテンツを追加」をタップ
② 画面上部に【15698】を入力しDoneをタップ

音声ストリーミング配信 》》》

この教科書の音声は、右記ウェブサイトにて無料で配信しています。

https://text.asahipress.com/free/english/

記事提供：CNN / The Japan Times / NIKKEI ASIAN REVIEW / Reuters / The Economist / VOA News / The Wall Street Journal / 朝日新聞社 / 共同通信社 / AP / AFP / 毎日新聞社 / 読売新聞社

写真提供：AP / CNN / iStock /KRT / The New York Times / アフロ / ロイター / AFP / WAA

表紙デザイン：大下賢一郎
本文イラスト：駿高泰子

English for Mass Communication — 2023 Edition —

は　し　が　き

　この本は、新聞・放送の英語ニュースをできるだけ多角的に学べるように編集したものです。

　時事英語を学ぶという行為は、「時事英語を理解すること」と「時事的な事柄や問題に関して英語でコミュニケーションを行うこと」の二つを学ぶことです。英語を読んだり、聞いたりすることは前者であり、時事的な事柄や問題に関して英語で書いたり、話したりすることが後者です。学習の順序としては、いうまでもなく、「理解」から入っていかなければなりません。英字新聞を読めず、英語放送を聞いてもよくわからない人が満足な英語を書けるはずがありませんし、話すことも期待できません。

　従って、この本の編集上の重点は、当然、「理解力の向上」に置かれています。この本では、政治・経済・外交・軍事・環境からスポーツにいたるまで多方面の英語ニュースを理解していただくように編集してあります。この教科書には授業の組み立て方に沿って色々な使い方があると思います。例えば、最もオーソドックスな使い方としては、まず時事英語の「理解力向上」に向けて二段階のアプローチをとることが可能です。まず第一段階として、英語ニュースを時事日本語に移しかえる能力を養うことです。そして第二段階でニュースの基本用語と英語ニュースの語学的特質を理解することです。従って、本書では各章において、まず、英語ニュースの読解と翻訳を行う構成となっています。そして、EXERCISE は、基本語学力を向上させることをねらいとしていますが、できるだけ「生きた英語」にアプローチしてもらうよう編集してあります。各章の News 記事にある「役立つ表現」（*Useful Expressions*）は Notes において☞で記されていますが、それらの表現を使って Exercise 1 の 2 で問題が設定されています。英語による発信力が求められる時代ですが、ニュース記事を読むだけではなく書く力を養成することにより、時代の要請に応える一助になればと思います。THE WORLD OF ENGLISH JOURNALISM は、主としてニュース英語の世界やニュース英語の語学的特質の理解を深めていただくために設けられています。また VOCABULARY BUILDUP は語彙力の充実をはかることをねらいとしています。この他にもいくつかの使い方があると思います。それぞれの授業の目標に即して最適な方法でお使い頂ければと思います。

　なお、本書における英語の綴りや句読点は、原則として、オリジナル記事の綴りに準拠しました。米国式・英国式で綴り方に違いがある場合も原文記事のままとし、必要に応じ注を加えてあります。例えば、「アメリカ合衆国」の略称は、米国式では U.S. となり、英国式では US となりますが、原文のままとしています。また、ニュース記事の冒頭における発信地の明示についても、内外のニュースを問わずオリジナル記事に準拠しました。

　本書の内容を一層充実させるため、読者諸氏のご教示を頂ければ幸いです。

　最後に、本書の出版にあたり種々のお骨折りを頂いた朝日出版社の日比野忠氏、加藤愛理氏、田所メアリー氏にこの場を借りて厚く御礼申し上げます。

編　著　者

CONTENTS

English for Mass Communication

NEWS 1

Disk 1

Japan ruling party wins big in polls in wake of Abe's death

Japan's governing party and its coalition partner scored a major victory in a parliamentary election Sunday amid uncertainty about how the assassination of former Prime Minister Shinzo Abe may affect party unity.

The Liberal Democratic Party and its junior coalition partner Komeito raised their combined share in the 248-seat chamber to 146—far beyond the majority—for 5 half of the seats in the less powerful upper house.

With the boost, Prime Minister Fumio Kishida stands to rule without interruption until a scheduled election in 2025. That would allow Kishida to work on long-term policies such as national security, his signature but still vague "new capitalism" economic policy, and his party's long-cherished goal to amend the U.S.-drafted 10 postwar pacifist constitution.

A charter change proposal is now a possibility. With the help of two opposition parties supportive of a charter change, the governing bloc now has the two-thirds majority in the chamber needed to propose an amendment, making it a realistic possibility. The governing bloc already has secured support in the other chamber. 15

Kishida welcomed the major win but wasn't smiling, given the loss of Abe and the hard task of unifying his party without him. In media interviews late Sunday, Kishida repeated, "Party unity is more important than anything else."

Kishida and senior party lawmakers observed a moment of silence for Abe at the party election headquarters before placing on the whiteboard victory ribbons next to 20 the names of candidates who secured their seats.

Abe, 67, was shot while giving a campaign speech in the western city of Nara on Friday and died of massive blood loss. He was Japan's longest-serving political leader over two terms in office, and though he stepped down in 2020 was deeply influential in the LDP while heading its largest faction, Seiwakai. Japan's current 25 diplomatic and security stance is unlikely to be swayed because fundamental changes had already been made by Abe.

He became Japan's youngest prime minister in 2006, at age 52. But his overly nationalistic first stint abruptly ended a year later, also because of his health, prompting six years of annual leadership change. He returned to office in 2012, 30 vowing to revitalize the nation and get its economy out of its deflationary doldrums with his "Abenomics" formula, which combined fiscal stimulus, monetary easing and structural reforms. He won six national elections and built a rock-solid grip on power.

— *Based on a report on AP News.com on July 11, 2022* —

〈ニュース解説〉 令和4年7月8日、歴代最長任期の総理大臣職を務めた安倍晋三氏が選挙遊説中に狙撃され、死亡するという未曽有の悲劇が発生した。その2日後に行われた参議院議員選挙の結果、与党自民党は改選議席の過半数を超える大勝を収め、憲法改正に前向きと言われる勢力は衆参合わせて3分の2を超えた。内外に重要課題が山積する中、安倍氏とは政治的スタンスに違いがあるとされる岸田文雄首相の政権運営は正念場を迎えることとなった。

(Notes) 【※☞マークは *Useful Expressions*】

☞◆ **Japan ruling party wins big in polls in wake of Abe's death** 「（日本の）与党（参院選）大勝 安倍氏の死去を受け」［"ruling party" は「与党」で後出 "governing party" も同義。"polls" はここでは選挙、投票の意。☞ "in the wake of" は「～の結果として」「～に続いて」。ここでは、英語ニュースの見出し "headline" のスタイルに従って冠詞が省かれている。"headline" は、本記事のように冒頭段落の "lead" を要約する場合や記事内容から新たに書き下ろす場合がある。即時性と簡潔さを尊び、過去の事象にも現在形を用いる等、独特のスタイルがある。P.13"THE WORLD OF ENGLISH JOURNALISM（The headline)" 参照］

◆ (L. 1) **coalition partner** 連立パートナー（相手）［後出 "junior coalition partner" は、「連立を組む（下位）パートナー」

◆ (L. 1-2) **major victory in a parliamentary election** （参議院）国政選挙における大勝［英語ニュースでは、日本の事情に疎い読者のため、国会（Diet）等の固有名称は出さず、英国などで一般的に「議会」を意味する "parliament" を使うことが多い。"major victory" の同義語には後出の "major win" や "landslide victory（圧勝)" などがある］

☞◆ (L. 2) **amid uncertainty about** ～の不確実性がある中

◆ (L. 2) **assassination** 暗殺

◆ (L. 3) **former Prime Minister Shinzo Abe** 安倍晋三元首相（「首相」は「内閣総理大臣」の通称。単に「総理」とも呼ばれる。"former" は「元」、「前」両方を意味するので、事実関係の確認が必要。故人の場合、「故」に相当する "late" も使われる）

◆ (L. 4) **Liberal Democratic Party** 自由民主党（略称 "LDP"）

◆ (L. 4) **Komeito** 公明党（正式英語名称 "Komeito Party"）

◆ (L. 5) **248-seat chamber** 定数248議席の議院（"Chamber" は "House" と同義でここでは参議院を指す）

◆ (L. 6) **less powerful upper house** （衆議院と比し）優越性を持たない参議院（"upper house" は「参議院（House of Councillors)」を英国の上院である「貴族院（House of Lords)」に擬した呼び方。「衆議院（House of Representatives)」は同様に下院である「庶民院（House of Commons)」になぞらえ "lower house" と呼ばれる。日本国憲法上、衆議院は、参議院に対し、内閣総理大臣指名、法案議決、予算案議決、条約議決等で優越性があることを指す）

◆ (L. 7) **with the boost** この議席増により

◆ (L. 7) **Prime Minister Fumio Kishida** 岸田文雄首相

◆ (L. 7-8) **rule without interruption until a scheduled election in 2025** 2025年（7月）に予定される次期参院選まで途切れることなく政権を維持できる［実際には衆議院の任期満了（同年10月21日）以前に解散・総選挙があればこの限りではない］

◆ (L. 9) **national security** 国家安全保障

◆ (L. 9-10) **signature but still vague "new capitalism" economic policy** （岸田首相の）看板（政策）だが依然内容が漠然としている「新しい資本主義」という経済政策（"signature" は「代表的な」「看板の」の意）

◆ (L. 10) **long-cherished goal** 長く維持してきた政策目標（改憲は自民党立党の主要目標の一つ）

◆ (L. 10-11) **amend the U.S.-drafted postwar pacifist constitution** （占領期に）米国が原案を起草した戦後平和主義憲法を改正する［"pacifist（平和主義)" はしばしば無抵抗主義を含意する］

◆ (L. 12-13) **two opposition parties supportive of a charter change** 憲法改正に前向きな2野党（日本維新の会及び国民民主党を指す。"charter" は "constitution" と同義で「憲法」を意味する）

◆ (L. 13-14) **two-thirds majority in the chamber** 参議院議席の3分の2の多数（憲法改正は衆参両院それぞれで3分の2以上の賛成で発議され、国民投票の過半数を得ることが必要）

◆ (L. 19) **observe a moment of silence for Abe** 安倍氏への黙とうを捧げる

◆ (L. 22) **the western city of Nara** （西日本の都市である）奈良市（"of" は同格を表す）

◆ (L. 23-24) **Japan's longest-serving political leader over two terms in office** 2つの期間を合わせ日本史上最長任期となる総理大臣職を務めた政治指導者

◆ (L. 25) **largest faction, Seiwakai** 最大派閥の清和会（正式名称「清和政策研究会」。安倍氏が会長だった。形がい化しつつある保守本流・傍流の別では傍流に属する。自民党内の派閥の役割は近時低下しているとされる）

◆ (L. 30) **six years of annual leadership change** 毎年のように首相が交代した6年間（安倍首相の1期目と2期目の間の6年間に5人の首相が就任していることを指す）

◆ (L. 31) **deflationary doldrums** デフレ不況

◆ (L. 32) **"Abenomics" formula** 「アベノミクス」という処方箋

◆ (L. 33) **build a rock-solid grip on power** 権力を揺るぎないものとする

1. 本文の内容と一致するものには T (True) を、一致しないものには F (False) を記せ。

(　　) (1) Japan's ruling camp won the Upper House elections with a thin majority despite the death of the former Prime Minister Shinzo Abe.

(　　) (2) With the result of the election, Prime Minister Fumio Kishida will likely rule till 2025, when the next election is scheduled.

(　　) (3) With the help of two opposition parties supportive of a charter change, the ruling bloc enjoys the two-thirds majority in both houses needed to propose an amendment on Japan's postwar pacifist constitution.

(　　) (4) Japan's basic stance toward diplomatic and security issues is likely to shift, although fundamental changes were already made by Shinzo Abe.

(　　) (5) The former premier's economic policy, known as "Abenomics," was designed to pull Japan out of its deflationary economy with a combination of fiscal stimulus, monetary easing and structural reforms.

2. 本文中に掲げた [*Useful Expressions*] を参照し、下記の語群を並び替えて空欄に適語を記し、日本語に合う英文を完成させよ。

(1) ウクライナでの紛争の結果として世界はエネルギーや食料品価格の高騰に苦しんでいる。

(　　) (　　) (　　) (　　) (　　) (　　) in Ukraine, the world suffers from soaring energy and food prices.

> conflict, 　　 In, 　　 of, 　　 the（2度使用する）, 　　 wake

(2) 台風の進路が不確実な中、いくつかの航空便が南の目的地に向かって出発した。

Some airliners departed for southern destinations (　　) (　　) (　　) (　　) (　　) (　　) the typhoon.

> about, 　　 amid, 　　 of, 　　 path, 　　 the, 　　 uncertainty

音声を聞き、下線部を補え。（２回録音されています。１回目はナチュラルスピード、２回目はスロースピードです。）

Natural
4
Slow
6

Japan plans a state funeral on September 27 for former Prime Minister Shinzo Abe who was shot to death at a campaign rally this month, (1) _____ said on Wednesday. An official decision will be made at a cabinet meeting on Friday, they added.

The site will be the Nippon Budokan, an arena originally built for the 1964 Tokyo Olympic Games that has since been (2) _____, as well as the site for a memorial service for World War II dead held every year on August 15.

Japanese Prime Minister Fumio Kishida said last week that Abe would be given a state funeral in recognition of being Japan's longest-serving prime minister as well as for his contributions to Japan and the world.

Natural
5
Slow
7

The last such state funeral for a former prime minister, in which the (3) _____, was held in 1967 for ex-premier Shigeru Yoshida. Costs for more recent funerals were borne half by the state and half by the ruling Liberal Democratic Party (LDP).

The (4) _____ Japan, with opponents objecting to the use of tax money and others saying the LDP is making political use of Abe's death.

An (5) _____ public broadcaster NHK found 49% of respondents in favour of the idea and 38% against. Those aged 18-39 were most in favour, at 61%, while those in their 60s were most against at 51%.

— *Based on a report on Reuters.com on July 20, 2022* —

5

10

15

20

〈ニュース解説〉　参議院選挙戦中の白昼、突然凶弾に倒れた安倍晋三元首相。連続在職 2822 日、通算在職 3188 日は、我が国憲政史上いずれも最長記録だ。安倍氏の業績については、意見の分かれるところもあるが、氏が提唱した「自由で開かれたインド太平洋（Free and Open Indo-Pacific）」構想は西側自由民主主義国における基本認識として定着した。G7 サミットなどでの活躍も特筆される。氏の逝去に当たり、150 を超える国・地域・機関の首脳から弔電が殺到するなど、その死を悼む声は大きく、岸田首相は、吉田茂氏以来となる国葬実施に踏み切った。

(Notes)
state funeral 国葬（政府は、正式には「国葬儀」と称し、一般の葬儀とは異なる政府主催の追悼儀式と位置付けた）　**cabinet meeting** 閣議　**site**（国葬の実施）会場　**the Nippon Budokan** 日本武道館　**the 1964 Tokyo Olympic Games** 1964 年のオリンピック東京大会　**memorial service for World War Ⅱ dead** 第二次世界大戦戦没者追悼式（正式名称「全国戦没者追悼式」）　**in recognition of** 〜の功績を讃え　**ex-premier Shigeru Yoshida** 吉田茂元首相（"ex-" は "former" 同様「元」を表す接頭辞）　**make political use of Abe's death** 安倍氏の死を政治利用する　**public broadcaster NHK** 公共放送の NHK（正式名称「日本放送協会」）　**in favour of** 〜に賛成して（"favour" は英国綴り）　**against** 〜に反対して

■問A 空所 (a) ～ (n) にそれぞれ入るべき1語を下記の語群から選びその番号を記せ。

内閣府	→	Cabinet (a)
防衛省	→	Ministry of (b)
金融庁	→	Financial Services (c)
法務省	→	Ministry of (d)
総務省	→	Ministry of Internal Affairs and (e)
財務省	→	Ministry of (f)
外務省	→	Ministry of Foreign (g)
環境省	→	Ministry of the (h)
文部科学省	→	Ministry of (i), Culture, Sports, Science and Technology
厚生労働省	→	Ministry of (j), Labour, and Welfare
農林水産省	→	Ministry of Agriculture, Forestry and (k)
経済産業省	→	Ministry of Economy, (l) and Industry
国土交通省	→	Ministry of Land, (m), Transport and Tourism
国家公安委員会	→	National Public Safety (n)

1. Affairs	2. Agency	3. Commission
4. Communications	5. Defense	6. Education
7. Environment	8. Finance	9. Fisheries
10. Health	11. Infrastructure	12. Justice
13. Office	14. Trade	

■問B (a) ～ (f) にそれぞれ対応する英語表現を下記の語群から選びその番号を記せ。

(a) 憲法　　(b) 国会　　(c) 総選挙　　(d) 与党　　(e) 野党　　(f) 連立

1. coalition	2. constitution	3. Diet
4. general election	5. opposition party	6. ruling party

■問C (a) ～ (j) にそれぞれ入るべき1語を下記の語群から選びその番号を記せ。

自由民主党	→ (a) Democratic Party	立憲民主党 → (b) Democratic Party of Japan
日本維新の会	→ Nippon (c) no Kai	公明党　　→ (d) Party
国民民主党	→ Democratic Party for the (e)	日本共産党 → Japanese (f) Party
小選挙区制	→ single-seat (g) system	比例代表制 → proportional (h) system
衆議院	→ House of (i)	参議院　　→ House of (j)

1. Communist	2. constituency	3. Constitutional	4. Councillors
5. Ishin	6. Komeito	7. Liberal	8. People
9. representation	10. Representatives		

News defined ― ニュースは記者が決める？

掲載するニュースを決めるのは編集局（記者）だが、ニュースの定義には、世の中に起こっているすべてがニュースだという考えもある。しかし他方で、そのような様々な出来事からニュースにする価値あり（newsworthy）と記者が判断して選んだものがニュースだという考えもある。記者たちの中には、"We determine the news!" と公言して、ニュースは記者が作るものだと考えている人たちも多い。また、ニュースを選ぶ基準として、"what people want to know" と "what people need to know" の間のバランスを取ることも大切である。

このトピックを英文で読んでみよう。

How do you determine whether a current idea, event or problem is news? How do you recognize it, separating swiftly the news and the non-news in what happens? How can you be sure that it will interest readers, listeners, or viewers?

To answer these questions, examine the elements common in all news. These may also be termed news values, appeals, factors, determinants, or criteria. Even if one is missing, the reporter may question whether the happening is news.

The five news elements are: (a) timeliness, (b) nearness, (c) size, (d) importance and (e) personal benefit.

NEWS 2

Disk 1 **IMF cuts global growth forecast due to "seismic waves" from Russia's war in Ukraine**

The International Monetary Fund on Tuesday slashed its forecast for global economic growth by nearly a full percentage point, citing Russia's war in Ukraine, and warning that inflation was now a "clear and present danger" for many countries.

The war is expected to further increase inflation, the IMF said in its latest World Economic Outlook, warning that a further tightening of Western sanctions on Russia ⁵ to target energy exports would cause another major drop in global output.

The IMF said other risks to the outlook include a sharper-than-expected deceleration in China prompted by a flare-up of COVID-19 lockdowns. Rising prices for food, energy and other goods could trigger social unrest, particularly in vulnerable developing countries, the IMF said. ₁₀

Downgrading its forecasts for the second time this year, the global crisis lender said it now projects global growth of 3.6% in both 2022 and 2023, a drop of 0.8 and 0.2 percentage point, respectively, from its January forecast due to the war's direct impacts on Russia and Ukraine and global spillovers.

Global growth is expected to decline to about 3.3% over the medium term, ₁₅ compared to an average of 4.1% in the period from 2004 to 2013, and growth of 6.1% in 2021. "What has Russia's invasion of Ukraine cost? A crisis on top of a crisis, with devastating human costs and a massive setback for the global economy," IMF Managing Director Kristalina Georgieva told a food security panel on Tuesday.

The IMF has estimated that Ukraine's GDP will collapse by 35% this year, while ₂₀ Russia's output will shrink by 8.5% in 2022, while emerging and developing Europe, including both countries, will contract by 2.9%. But IMF Chief economist Pierre-Olivier Gourinchas told a news briefing that a tightening of sanctions against Russia to include restrictions on energy exports could double Russia's GDP decline to 17% by 2023. ₂₅

Spillovers from higher energy prices, a loss of confidence and financial market turmoil from this step would cut another two percentage points off of global growth forecasts, Gourinchas said.

The European Union, highly dependent on Russian energy, saw its 2022 growth forecast cut by 1.1 percentage points, while Britain now faces slower economic ₃₀ growth and more persistent inflation than any other major economy next year.

The war has exacerbated inflation that already had been rising in many countries due to imbalances in supply and demand linked to the pandemic, with the latest lockdowns in China likely to cause new bottlenecks in global supply chains.

— Based on a report on Reuters.com on April 19, 2022 —

〈ニュース解説〉　世界経済の実質成長率は、新型コロナウイルス禍による経済活動の停滞で 2020 年にマイナス 3.1％と戦後最悪のマイナス成長に陥った。21 年にはデルタ株などの変異株が登場するが、ワクチン接種の進展、コロナ禍により先送りされた需要も取り込んだビジネス活動の再開、各国が導入した経済対策などにより、成長率は 6.1％と急回復した。ただし、需要増と供給制約の影響でインフレ圧力が上昇に転じた。22 年 2 月、ロシアがウクライナに侵攻した結果、原油や天然ガスなどの資源や小麦などの食料品が値上がりし、世界的にインフレがさらに加速した。こうした中、IMF は 22 年 4 月発行の "World Economic Outlook"（『世界経済見通し』）で世界経済の実質成長率予測を 1 月時点の 4.4％から 3.6％に引き下げると共に、世界経済に対するリスク要因として、コロナウイルス変異型の感染拡大、インフレの長期化、米国を始めとする各国の財政出動の縮小などを挙げた。また、22 年 7 月末には IMF は歴史的なインフレ、それに対応する米欧の利上げ、中国の「ゼロコロナ」政策によるロックダウン（都市封鎖）の継続などが追加のマイナス要因になるとして、22 年の予測値を 3.2％に再度引き下げた。

(Notes)　【※☞マークは *Useful Expressions*】

◆ **IMF**　国際通貨基金（International Monetary Fund）［1945 年に設立され、第 2 次世界大戦後の世界経済を支えてきた。国際金融と為替相場の安定化を目指す国連の専門機関。2022 年 3 月現在の加盟国 190 か国。本部：米ワシントン D.C.。IMF は毎年 4 月と 10 月に "World Economic Outlook"（世界経済見通し：略称 WEO）を発行し、重要な変化がある場合は適宜、改定が加えられる］

◆ **forecast**　（ここでは名詞として用いられているが、動詞の場合の過去と過去分詞形は forecasted と forecast の両方があることに注意）

◆ **seismic waves**　広範な影響（WEO からの引用。直訳は「地震波」）

◆ **Russia's war in Ukraine**　（本ニュースが報じられた 2022 年 4 月 19 日時点までのロシアのウクライナ侵攻の概況は次の通り：ロシアがウクライナ北部と国境を接するベラルーシに約 10 万人の地上部隊を集結し、ウクライナ侵攻を開始したのが 2022 年 2 月 24 日。数日後には、国境から 90 キロの首都キーウを包囲、数週間後にはウクライナ全土を制圧すると見られた。しかし、ウクライナ軍の予想外に激しい戦闘が 1 カ月以上続いた後、ロシア軍は 4 月初めまでにキーウ州全域から部隊を撤退し、4 月中旬には東部ルガンスク、ドネツク州の全域や、2014 年に一方的に併合したクリミア半島と両州をつなぐ南東部へ戦力再配備を進めた）

☞◆ (L. 2)　**percentage point**　パーセンテージポイント、ポイント（2 つのパーセントで示された数値の差。例えば、5％と 10％の差は five percent ではなく、five percentage points）

◆ (L. 3)　**"clear and present danger"**　明確にして差し迫った危険（本ニュースでは差し迫るインフレの脅威に言及しており、IMF 主任エコノミストが記者会見で用いた表現で引用符が付されている。この表現自体が最初に使われたのは 1919 年に米国連邦最高裁が下した判決で、「言論の自由」は基本的には制約してはならないが、何らかの即時かつ明かに重大な危険が生じ、公共の利益が損なわれると判断される場合には、その限りにあらず、というもの。「明白かつ現在の危険」と訳されることが多い）

◆ (L. 4)　**inflation**　インフレーション、インフレ（一般的に物価水準が持続的に上昇すること）

◆ (L. 5)　**Western sanctions on Russia**　西側諸国による対ロ制裁（前置詞として against も使われる）

◆ (L. 6)　**global output**　世界の GDP（国内総生産）［経済ニュース等では output はしばしば GDP（gross domestic product）の意味で使われる］

◆ (L. 11)　**for the second time this year**　（IMF は 2021 年 10 月に 22 年の世界の GDP 成長率を 4.9％と予測。22 年 1 月にはこれを 4.4％に引き下げると共に、23 年の成長率を 3.8％と予測した。今回、両年の予測値を共に 3.6％に改定した）

◆ (L. 11)　**global crisis lender**　グローバル（規模の金融）危機を回避する（最後の）貸し手［IMF には、加盟国が財政危機に陥り、他に資金供給を行う主体がいない場合に「最後の貸し手」（lender of last resort）として緊急融資をする機能があり、世界の中央銀行と呼ばれることもある］

☞◆ (L. 14)　**spillover(s)**　波及効果、波及現象［例えば、「〜からの波及効果」は spillover(s) from 〜（L.27 を参照）、「〜への波及効果」は spillover(s) into 〜などと表現される］

◆ (L. 15)　**medium-term**　中期の［おおよその目途は「短期」（short-term）が一年以内、「中期」が 1 年を超えて 3 〜 5 年、長期（long-term）が 5 年以上。22 年 4 月発行の WEO を参照すると、3.3％は 2027 年の予測として示されている。5 年先を「中期」と呼んでいることになる］

◆ (L. 18-19)　**IMF Managing Director Kristalina Georgieva**　IMF 専務理事クリスタリナ・ゲオルギエバ

◆ (L. 22-23)　**IMF Chief economist Pierre-Olivier Gourinchas**　IMF 主任エコノミスト、ピエール・オリビエ・グランシャ

◆ (L. 23)　**news briefing**　メディアブリーフィング（報道機関などに対して行われる簡単な事情説明。news conference と同義の場合もある）

◆ (L. 29)　**European Union**　欧州連合（略称：EU。ヨーロッパを中心に現在 27 か国が加盟する政治・経済統合体。現在、19 か国が欧州単一通貨ユーロ（Euro）を使用。（2023 年 1 月からクロアチアが Euro を導入予定で参加国は 20 へ。英国は 2020 年 1 月に EU を離脱）

☞◆ (L. 34)　**bottleneck(s) in 〜**　〜に関わる（ボトル）ネック、障害、隘路

1. 本文の内容と一致するものには T (True) を、一致しないものには F (False) を記せ。

(   ) (1) The latest World Economic Outlook cautions that the tightening of energy exports to Russia from Western countries will result in another significant drop in global GDP.

(   ) (2) The IMF believes that China's economy will suffer more than forecasted if Covid-19 lockdowns continue to spread.

(   ) (3) The IMF cut its forecast of global growth in 2022 and 2023 for the second time in 2022, amid concern about the war in Ukraine hurting the economies of Russia, Ukraine and elsewhere.

(   ) (4) Medium-term global growth is likely to fall to about 3.3%, with IMF's managing director attributing a huge setback for global growth to Russia's invasion of Ukraine.

(   ) (5) In its latest review, the IMF predicts Ukraine will suffer greater contraction than Russia, because Russia is likely to restrict its energy exports to Ukraine.

2. 本文中に掲げた［*Useful Expressions*］を参照し、下記の語群を並び替えて空欄に適語を記し、日本語に合う英文を完成させよ。

(1) その企業の昨年の売上高利益率は 10％だったが、本年は 15％に上昇する見込みで、5（パーセンテージ）ポイントの改善は高収益の新商品投入に起因する。

The company's profit-to-sales ratio was 10 percent last year, while it is predicted to rise to 15 percent this year, with the markup of (   ) (   ) (   ) (   ) (   ) the introduction of highly profitable new products.

> attributed   five   percentage   points   to

(2) 世界経済はこの革新的な技術から有益な波及効果を享受することになろう。

The global economy is expected to (   ) (   ) (   ) (   ) (   ) (   ) technology.

> enjoy   from   innovative   positive   spillovers   this

(3) 自動車メーカーは生産コストをさらに低減すべく、生産ラインのボトルネックを見つけて除去しようと努めている。

The car maker is making efforts to (   ) (   ) (   ) (   ) (   ) its production line, aiming to lower production costs further.

> and   bottlenecks   eliminate   identify   in

音声を聞き、下線部を補え。（2回録音されています。1回目はナチュラルスピード、2回目はスロースピードです。）

Natural 10
Slow 12

　　　This has been the worst start to a year for stocks in more than half a century. A record-setting run fueled by cheap money has ended, and Wall Street is having a hard time adjusting to a new reality. With the Federal Reserve aggressively hiking interest rates to fight high inflation, ⁽¹⁾＿＿＿＿＿＿＿＿＿＿＿＿＿＿＿＿＿.

　　　At the halfway point of the year, the tech-heavy Nasdaq has fallen by 30% and the broad-based S&P 500 is down by over 20%. Both indexes are in bear market territory, and the Dow Jones Industrial Average is in a correction. Year to date, it is down over 15%.

　　　"When interest rates go up, it changes all the math," says Charles Bobrinskoy, vice chairman of Ariel Investments. "It ⁽²⁾＿＿＿＿＿＿＿＿＿＿＿＿＿, buying a house, buying a bond, and it changes the value of particularly tech stocks, whose earnings are far off in the future."

Natural 11
Slow 13

　　　And that means that all that whipsawing on Wall Street of the last few months—including the massive single-day swings of more than 1,000 points—⁽³⁾＿＿＿＿＿＿＿＿＿＿＿＿＿. They're worried the Fed may tip the U.S. economy into a recession.

　　　While that volatility has been driven mainly by rising interest rates and inflation, it has been ⁽⁴⁾＿＿＿＿＿＿＿＿＿＿＿: COVID-19 continues to wreak havoc and lockdowns in China, global supply chains remain clogged and Russia's invasion of Ukraine continues.

　　　The Federal Reserve is ⁽⁵⁾＿＿＿＿＿＿＿＿＿＿＿ and policymakers are aware there are risks. If the Fed's interest rate increases cool the economy too much, it could lead to a deep downturn and even a recession. Even Fed Chair Jerome Powell doesn't discount that.

— Based on a report on npr. org on June 30, 2022 —

〈ニュース解説〉　本ニュースは米国経済の 2022 年前半の状況を株価、金利、インフレの観点から報じている。米国の主要株価指数、ダウ工業株 30 種平均はリーマン・ショック後の 2009 年 2 月末に約 7100 ドルに急落したが、米連邦準備理事会（FRB）のゼロ金利政策が奏功し、2021 年 11 月末には約 34500 ドルへと大幅に上昇した。一方、コロナ禍からの需要回復と供給制約で 2021 年 5 月頃からインフレが急伸、FRB は鎮静化を狙って 2022 年 3 月、5 月に政策金利を 0.25 ポイント、0.5 ポイント引き上げた後、6 月、7 月にも立て続けに 0.75 ポイントずつ引き上げた。しかし、インフレは 7 月時点でも高止まりしており、9 月に再度 0.75 ポイント引き上げられる可能性がある。このインフレには、米国や中国のコロナ禍に加え、ロシアのウクライナ侵攻などに起因する供給制約も絡んでいるが、エコノミストの間では "true nature of the current inflation bout"（現下のインフレ高進の本質）が「一過性」なのか、「持続的」なのかに関して盛んに議論が戦わされている。その背景には、欧米経済が成熟し、日本経済にみられる長期停滞が常態化することへの強い警戒感がある。今回のインフレ高騰をいち早く予測したサマーズ元米財務長官は、米国経済がコロナ禍やウクライナ危機前の低インフレ・低金利に戻る確率を 6 割と予測している。

(Notes)
run（株価の）上昇局面　**cheap money** 低金利資金　**Federal Reserve (Board)** 連邦準備（制度）理事会（米国の中央銀行。略称：FRB 英文メディアでは初出は "Federal Reserve"、その後は "the Fed"、邦字紙では初出は「連邦準備（制度）理事会」、その後は「FRB」とするのが一般的）　**tech-heavy Nasdaq** ハイテク株が多いナスダック総合株価指数（National Association of Securities Dealers Automated Quotations の略称）　**broad-based S&P 500**（米国経済を）幅広く代表する（500 銘柄で構成する）S&P500 種指数　**bear market territory** 弱気相場の領域　**Dow Jones Industrial Average** ダウ工業株 30 種平均（米国を代表する 30 銘柄で構成される株価指数）　**correction** 調整局面（長期間上昇した株価が再度上昇、または下落する前に踊り場に入った状況）　**year to date** 年初来　**Charles Bobrinskoy, vice chairman of Ariel Investments** アリエル・インベストメンツのチャールズ・ボブリンスコイ副会長　**bond** 債券　**tech stock** ハイテク株　**earnings** 利益、収益　**whipsawing** 乱高下　**swings of more than 1,000 points** 1000 ドルを超す変動（米国の株価指標は point で表記される）　**tip ~ into a recession** ~を景気後退に追い込む　**volatility** 相場変動　**lockdown** 都市封鎖（動詞が wreak であることに注意）　**supply chain** 供給網　**policymakers** 政策策定者、政策当局（ここでは FRB を指す）　**Fed Chair Jerome Powell** ジェローム・パウエル米連邦準備（制度）理事会議長

■問A 空所 (a) ～ (s) にそれぞれ入るべき1語を下記の語群から選びその番号を記せ。

国内総生産	→	(a) domestic product
消費者物価指数	→	(b) price index
卸売物価指数	→	(c) price index
非関税障壁	→	non-tariff (d)
最恵国	→	most (e) nation
政府開発援助	→	(f) development assistance
貿易不均衡	→	trade (g)
為替レート	→	(h) rate
国際収支	→	(i) of international payments
経常収支	→	current (j)
貿易自由化	→	trade (k)
社会保障	→	social (l)
企業の合併・買収	→	(m) and acquisition
株式公開買い付け	→	(n) bid
店頭取引株	→	over-the-(o) stock
優良株	→	(p) chip
不良債権	→	(q) loan
失業率	→	(r) rate
住宅着工件数	→	(s) starts

1. account	2. bad	3. balance	4. barrier
5. blue	6. consumer	7. counter	8. exchange
9. favored	10. gross	11. housing	12. imbalance
13. jobless	14. liberalization	15. merger	16. official
17. security	18. takeover	19. wholesale	

■問B (a) ～ (d) をそれぞれ和訳せよ。

(a) European Central Bank

(b) Bank of Japan

(c) Federal Reserve Board

(d) New York Stock Exchange

■問C (a) ～ (d) にそれぞれ対応する英語を下記の語群から選びその番号を記せ。

(a) 景気後退　　(b) 好況　　(c) 倒産　　(d) 年金

| 1. bankruptcy | 2. bonus | 3. boom | 4. breakdown |
| 5. pension | 6. recession | 7. rehabilitation | |

The headline ―「見出し」の特徴

現代英文ジャーナリズムの「見出し」（headline）では、日常的に用いられない語を「見出し語」（headlinese）として使用することを避ける傾向が強い。見出しは記事の内容を簡潔明瞭に表現する必要があり、一般的に次の5つの特徴を有している。

（1）略語が多い。例えば、"GOP" と言えば "Grand Old Party" の略称で、米国共和党（Republican Party）の異名。

（2）特殊記号がある。例えば、"and" をカンマで代用したり、情報源を表すコロンがある。ヘッドラインのコロンはすべて情報源を表すものではないが、"Gunman in Manhattan kills one woman, wounds three: NYPD" とあれば、カンマは "and" に置き換えて "Gunman in Manhattan kills one woman and wounds three" となり、この情報は NYPD（New York City Police Department, ニューヨーク市警察）によってもたらされたことがわかる。

（3）冠詞や be 動詞は省略されることが多い。

（4）見出しにとどまらず、英語ニュースでは、首都名はその国や政府を表すことが多い。例えば、Washington は米国や米国政府を表す場合がよくある。もちろん首都自体のことを表す場合もあるから、文脈に注意。

（5）時制のずらしに気をつけよう。昨日起こったことでも現在形で表現。未来は to 不定詞で表現。例えば見出し語で "Government to regulate the Internet" とあれば、"The government will regulate the Internet" の意味。

このトピックを英文で読んでみよう。

The modern headline is distinguished by the fact that it says something—it makes a complete statement instead of merely characterizing. But, in addition, it speaks a language of its own. This language is not "headlinese," a perverted speech, but is merely pure English adapted to the requirements of headlining.

For one thing, the present tense is customarily used to describe past events. This usage is not something created by headline writers, but is simply something borrowed from everyday speech. The present tense is employed because it is the tense of immediacy, because it is more vivid and, hence, because it makes our trial tube of toothpaste inviting to the prospective buyer.

Another characteristic, which is more obvious to the ordinary reader, is the omission of non-essential words, chiefly articles. This practice has a tendency to give the headline telegraphic speed and, hence, to make it more vivid.

Still another characteristic of headline language is the use of short words, mainly of Anglo-Saxon derivation. And, here again, the space requirement is the commanding factor.

NEWS 3

Disk 1
(14)

Japan's economy shrank 1 percent as consumers fled Covid

TOKYO—Last December, after two years of stop-and-go growth, Japan's economic engine seemed like it might finally be revving up. Covid cases were practically nonexistent. Consumers were back on the town, shopping, eating out, traveling. The year 2021 ended on a high note, with the country's economy expanding on an annual basis for the first time in three years.　　　5

But the Omicron variant of the coronavirus, geopolitical turmoil and supply chain snarls have once again set back Japan's fragile economic recovery. In the first three months of the year, the country's economy, the world's third largest after the United States and China, shrank at an annualized rate of 1 percent, government data showed on Wednesday.　　　10

A combination of factors contributed to the decline in growth. In January, Japan had put into place new emergency measures as coronavirus case numbers, driven up by Omicron, moved toward the highest levels of the pandemic. In February, Russia invaded Ukraine, spiking energy prices. And that was before China, Japan's largest export market and a key supplier of parts and labor to its manufacturers, imposed　15 new lockdowns in Shanghai, throwing supply chains into chaos.

(15)　The contraction has not been as "extreme" as previous economic setbacks thanks to high levels of vaccine uptake and less wide-ranging emergency measures than during previous waves of the coronavirus, according to Shinichiro Kobayashi, principal economist at the Mitsubishi UFJ Research Institute.　　　20

Growth is likely to bounce back strongly in the second quarter, analysts said, a pattern that has defined Japan's economy during the pandemic: Demand has waxed as Covid cases have waned, and vice versa.

Still, growth in the coming months will face some tough challenges. The pandemic and the war in Ukraine have fueled big increases in the costs of food and　25 energy in Japan. And moves by the U.S. Federal Reserve to tackle high inflation have caused the value of the Japanese currency, the yen, to plummet. That has driven up costs in the resource-poor country, which is highly dependent on imports for food, fuel and raw materials.

Inflation in the country, while still modest, is rising at its fastest pace in years,　30 with consumer prices in Tokyo increasing by 2.5 percent in April. And over the last year, prices for producers have shot up 10 percent, the highest levels since 1980.

— Based on a report on nytimes.com on May 17, 2022 —

〈ニュース解説〉　本ニュースは 2022 年 5 月時点で日本経済が直面する難局を報じており、その要因は NEWS 2 が伝える世界経済が抱える諸問題と重なる部分が多い。コロナ禍、ウクライナ危機、中国の都市封鎖に起因する供給制約が深刻なインフレ圧力を生みだしているという構図である。これに本ニュースにある「円安」という要因を加えれば、ほぼ日本の状況になる。ただし、もう一点、重要な情報が提供されている。それは、22 年 4 月の消費者物価指数の上昇率 2.5％に対して、企業物価指数の上昇率が約 10％というおそらく他先進国では例を見ない乖離である。賃金が上がらないために消費者の需要が弱い、企業は原料高を十分に価格に転嫁できず利益が伸びないため賃上げもできない、という日本経済が抱える悪循環だ。

(Notes)

◆　(L. 1)　**stop-and-go**　停止と発進を繰り返す

◆　(L. 3)　**on the town**　（特に、夜に）町へ繰り出す

◆　(L. 4)　**on a high note**　成功裏に、楽しく

◆　(L. 6)　**Omicron variant of the coronavirus**　新型コロナウイルスの変異型「オミクロン株」

◆　(L. 7)　**snarl**　障害、目詰まり、分断

☞◆　(L. 11)　**a combination of factors contributed to** …　複数の要因が絡んで … の原因となった

◆　(L. 12)　**new emergency measures**　新たな緊急措置（ここでは、「緊急事態宣言」に比べて制限の範囲やレベルを絞る「まん延防止等重点措置」を指している）

◆　(L. 16)　**Shanghai**　上海市（中国の商業・金融・工業などの中心地で、人口 2600 万余りで中国最大の都市）

☞◆　(L. 16)　**throwing supply chains into chaos**　サプライチェインを混乱に落しこむ（throw somebody/something into confusion/chaos/disarray といった表現でしばしば使われる）

◆　(L. 18)　**vaccine uptake**　ワクチン接種率（vaccination rate も同義）

◆　(L. 19)　**Shinichiro Kobayashi**　小林真一郎［三菱総合研究所（Mitsubishi UFJ Research Institute）主席研究員］

◆　(L. 22)　**define**　〜を特徴付ける

☞◆　(L. 28)　**highly dependent on imports for food**　食料に関して輸入への依存度がかなり高い（dependent on 〜 for … は成句。動詞として用いる場合には depend on 〜 for …）

◆　(L. 31)　**consumer prices**　消費者物価［消費者物価指数は Consumer Price Index（CPI）］

◆　(L. 32)　**prices for producers**　企業物価指数［Corporate Goods Price Index（CGPI）。企業間で取引する財の価格が対象。米国などでは Producer Price Index（PPI）が用いられる］

1. 本文の内容と一致するものには T (True) を、一致しないものには F (False) を記せ。

(　) (1) Japan's economy achieved, through ups and downs, annualized growth for two consecutive years until 2021.

(　) (2) An economic loss resulting from surging Omicron infections was a reason behind Japan's economy ranking third after those of the U.S. and China in early 2022.

(　) (3) After new lockdowns in Shanghai, the resulting supply chain disruptions were soon eased, thanks to help given by Japanese manufacturers there.

(　) (4) In the first three months of the year, Japan's economy suffered less than before, helped by more people receiving Covid-19 vaccination and more targeted Covid-19 emergency measures.

(　) (5) During the pandemic, Japan's economy has shown a tendency for its second-quarter GDP to improve over its first-quarter's.

2. 本文中に掲げた［*Useful Expressions*］を参照し、下記の語群を並び替えて空欄に適語を記し、日本語に合う英文を完成させよ。

(1) 協力者達の技能と経験が相俟って、これまでにない結果が生み出された。

A (　) (　) (　) (　) (　) held by the collaborators (　) (　) to unprecedented results.

> and　combination　contributed　experience　has　of　skills

(2) 参加者の一人による予想外の発言でその会議は大混乱に陥った。

An unexpected remark made by one of the participants (　) (　) (　) (　) (　) (　).

> confusion　into　meeting　the　threw　total

(3) 今日の世界は、かつて人間が行っていた日常の職務の遂行でロボットへの依存を益々高めている。

Today's world has grown (　) (　) (　) (　) (　) (　) routine tasks that used to be done by humans.

> dependent　for　increasingly　on　performing　robots

音声を聞き、下線部を補え。（２回録音されています。１回目はナチュラルスピードです。２回目はスロースピードです。）

Natural
16

Slow
18

Natural
17

Slow
19

Russian President Vladimir Putin has handed full control over a major oil and natural gas project partly owned by Shell and two Japanese companies to a newly created Russian firm, (1) _____ with the West over Moscow's military action in Ukraine.

Putin's decree late Thursday orders the creation of a new company that would take over ownership of Sakhalin Energy Investment Co., which (2) _____ British energy giant Shell and Japan-based Mitsui and Mitsubishi.

Putin's order named "threats to Russia's national interests and its economic security" as the reason for the move at Sakhalin-2, one of the world's largest export-oriented oil and natural gas projects. The presidential order (3) _____ if they want to retain the same shares in the new company.

Russian state-controlled natural gas giant Gazprom had a controlling stake in Sakhalin-2, the country's first offshore gas project that (4) _____ for liquefied natural gas, or LNG. Japan, South Korea and China are the main customers for the project's oil and LNG exports.

Shell (5) _____. After the start of the Russian military action in Ukraine, Shell announced its decision to pull out of all of its Russian investments, a move that it said has cost at least $5 billion.

Seiji Kihara, deputy chief secretary of the Japanese cabinet, said the government was aware of Putin's decree and was reviewing its impact. Japan-based Mitsui owns 12.5% of the project, and Mitsubishi holds 10%. Kihara emphasized that the project should not be undermined because it "is pertinent to Japan's energy security," adding that "anything that harms our resource rights is unacceptable."

— *Based on an AP report on VOANews.com on July 1, 2022* —

〈ニュース解説〉「サハリン2」は液化天然ガス（LNG）を年1000万トン生産し、日本向けに約600万トン（日本のLNG輸入量の約1割）を輸出する重要な供給ソース。運営会社サハリン・エナジーにはロシア国営ガスプロム、英国シェル、日本の三井物産、三菱商事が出資する。2022年2月のロシアによるウクライナ侵攻を受けて、シェルは3月初旬、ロシア事業からの完全撤退の意向を表明、外国企業と権益売却交渉を進めていると報じられた。6月末、ロシアのプーチン大統領はサハリン2の運営を新たな会社に移管する大統領令を発効させ、8月5日に新会社「サハリンスカヤ・エネルギヤ」が設立された。既存の株主は1カ月以内に参画の意思を知らせるよう求められ、三井、三菱両社は参画を申請し、8月末までにロシア政府から承認を得たが、シェルは改めて撤退を表明。日本2社の新会社傘下に不利な条件は見当たらないと報じられているが、詳細な条件交渉はこれからで、事業の主導権をロシア側が握ることへの懸念はなお残る。9月5日、ロシア大統領府は「西側諸国」がウクライナ侵攻を巡る対ロ制裁を解除するまで、ガスパイプライン「ノルドストリーム」による欧州向け供給の全面再開はしないと発表した。日本も不測の事態への備えが重要である。（2022年9月初め時点）

(Notes)
Vladimir Putin ウラジーミル・プーチン（ロシア連邦第2・4代大統領）　**Shell** シェル（石油・天然ガスなどのエネルギー関連事業を展開する英国の多国籍企業。正式名：Shell plc）　**the West** 西側諸国、西欧諸国　**Moscow** モスクワ（ロシア連邦の首都。ここでは「ロシア政府」の意）　**Ukraine** ウクライナ　**Sakhalin Energy Investment Co.** サハリン・エナジー・インベストメント［サハリン2の運営会社、本社：サハリン州ユジノサハリンスク。株主：ガスプロム（50％＋1株）、シェル（27.5％−1株）、三井物産（12.5％）、三菱商事（10％）]　**Mitsui** 三井物産　**Mitsubishi** 三菱商事　**Sakhalin-2** サハリン2［前出のサハリン・エナジーが運営する石油・ガス複合開発事業。LNG (liquefied natural gas「液化天然ガス」）生産能力は年間960万トンで約6割を日本に供給。日本に地理的に近く、エネルギー安全保障上の意義が大きい]　**presidential order** 大統領令　**Gazprom** ガスプロム（ロシア国営ガス会社）　**controlling stake** 支配持ち分（発行済株式の過半数を意味し、株主総会の意思決定とその執行に影響力を及ぼす）　**offshore gas project** 海底ガス田プロジェクト　**Seiji Kihara, deputy chief secretary of the Japanese cabinet** 木原誠二内閣官房副長官　**resource rights** 資源権益

■問A　空所 (a) ～ (s) にそれぞれ入るべき 1 語を下記の語群から選びその番号を記せ。

グローバル人材	→	globally (a) human resources
重厚長大産業	→	(b) industry
終身雇用	→	(c) employment
熟練労働者	→	(d) worker
年功序列昇進制度	→	(e)-based promotion system
能力主義昇進制度	→	(f)-based promotion system
食料自給率	→	food (g)-sufficiency rate
初任給	→	(h) salary
人材派遣会社	→	(i)-employment agency
数値目標	→	(j) target
正社員	→	(k) employee
契約社員	→	(l) employee
設備投資	→	(m) investment
先行指標	→	(n) indicator
遅行指標	→	(o) indicator
一致指標	→	(p) indicator
知的所有権	→	intellectual (q) rights
確定給付型年金	→	defined-(r) pension plan
確定拠出型年金	→	defined-(s) pension plan

1. benefit	2. capital	3. coincident	4. competitive
5. contract	6. contribution	7. full-time	8. lagging
9. leading	10. lifetime	11. numerical	12. performance
13. property	14. self	15. seniority	16. skilled
17. smokestack	18. starting	19. temporary	

■問B　(a) ～ (d) をそれぞれ和訳せよ。

(a) Asian Infrastructure Investment Bank

(b) Government Pension Investment Fund, Japan

(c) Japan External Trade Organization

(d) National Federation of Agricultural Cooperative Associations

■問C　(a) ～ (d) にそれぞれ対応する英語表現を下記の語群から選びその番号を記せ。

(a) 格安航空会社　　(b) 投資収益率　　(c) 有効求人倍率　　(d) 連結決算

1. consolidated earnings	2. effective labor force	3. low-cost carrier
4. ratio of job offers to seekers	5. return on investment	6. ultra-low airfare

The inverted pyramid — 逆ピラミッドとは

英文のニュースの大半は、ハード・ニュース（hard news）と呼ばれ、経済・政治・犯罪・事故・災害などに関連して日々起こる重要な出来事をスピーディーかつ簡潔に読者に伝える内容となっている。新聞の読者、テレビやラジオの視聴者、さらにはインターネットの利用者にとって時間は最も貴重な資源であり、多くの人たちは限られた時間内に最大限の情報を入手する必要に迫られている。こうしたニーズに対応するために考案されたのが逆ピラミッド型と呼ばれるニュースの構成であり、Chapter 6 で紹介するフィーチャー・ニュース（feature news）の構成と対比される。

このトピックを英文で読んでみよう。

This news writing format summarizes the most important facts at the very start of the story. It may seem like an obvious idea to us nowadays—getting right to the point when you start a story—but it did not occur to most reporters until midway through the 19th century. What changed? Sentences got shorter. Writing got tighter. And reporters developed a formula for compressing the most newsworthy facts—the who, what, when, where, why—into the opening paragraphs of a story. That formula lives on today. It is known as the inverted pyramid.

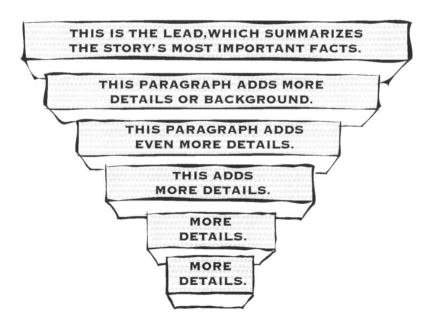

THIS IS THE LEAD, WHICH SUMMARIZES THE STORY'S MOST IMPORTANT FACTS.

THIS PARAGRAPH ADDS MORE DETAILS OR BACKGROUND.

THIS PARAGRAPH ADDS EVEN MORE DETAILS.

THIS ADDS MORE DETAILS.

MORE DETAILS.

MORE DETAILS.

NEWS 4

Disk 1
(20)

G7: China urged to press Russia to stop Ukraine war

G7 leaders urged China on Tuesday to use its influence with Russia to stop its invasion of Ukraine and drop "expansive maritime claims" in the South China Sea, in unprecedentedly tough criticism of Beijing's policies and human rights record.

They called on China to press Russia to pull forces out of Ukraine immediately and unconditionally, citing a ruling by the International Court of Justice that Moscow 5 suspend its military operation, and related UN General Assembly resolutions.

China says sanctions on Russia cannot resolve the Ukraine crisis and has criticised the United States and its allies for supplying arms to Ukraine.

"G7 countries only make up 10% of the world's population. They have no right to represent the world or to think their values and standards should apply to the 10 world," Chinese foreign ministry spokesman Zhao Lijian told a press briefing on Wednesday, when asked about the G7 communique.

(21) In the communique, concluding their three-day summit in the Bavarian Alps, the Group of Seven rich industrial democracies took aim at what they called coercive Chinese non-market policies that distorted the global economy. 15

The Chinese section of the communique, highlighted by the United States, referred to China's "non-transparent and market-distorting interventions" and other forms of economic and industrial directives.

The communique further voiced serious disquiet about the situation in the East and South China seas and unilateral attempts to change the status quo by force or 20 coercion.

It also said the G7 was now "gravely concerned"—a term not used in their summit a year ago—about the human rights situation in China, including forced labour in Tibet and Xinjiang. China should also honour its commitments to uphold rights, freedom and a high degree of autonomy in Hong Kong, they said. 25

A NATO summit starting immediately after the G7 summit will tackle China's deepening ties with Russia since Moscow's invasion of Ukraine and what is seen as Beijing's growing inclination to flex geopolitical muscle abroad.

— Based on a report on Reuters.com on June 28, 2022 —

〈ニュース解説〉 西側主要国首脳による 2022 年の G7 サミットが、ドイツ南部で開催された。議題の中心をなす安全保障問題の議論では、ロシアと連携を深める中国に対し、ウクライナ侵攻の終結のため、ロシアに圧力をかけることを要求。中国自身に対しても、覇権主義的な海洋進出や、人権抑圧等に深刻な懸念を表明した。引き続きスペインで NATO 首脳会合が開かれるなど、ウクライナ紛争のインパクトは安全保障への関心を近年になく高めることになった。

(Notes) 【※☞マークは *Useful Expressions*】

◆ **G7: China urged to press Russia to stop Ukraine war** 「G7　中国にロシアへの圧力を要求　ウクライナ戦争終結のため」["Ukraine war" ウクライナ戦争。正確には "lead" 記載の通りロシアによるウクライナ侵攻を指すが、"headline" 用法に従い、端的な表現に言い換えている。"：(コロン)" も同様で、コロンの前の主体(ここでは G7)が述べた内容を簡潔に引用している。G7 は後出 "Group of Seven(先進 7 国)" の略称。その「首脳(Leaders)」による "G7 Summit" の「サミット」は「頂上会談」の意。1975 年、仏開催の G5(先進 5 か国：米日英仏独)首脳会合で初出。後に伊及び加が参加し G7(先進 7 か国)に拡大。冷戦期にはソ連等東側諸国に対抗する西側の政治・経済上の包括的会議体となった。ソ連崩壊後の 1991 年からゴルバチョフ大統領など歴代ロシア首脳が非公式に招待されていたが、1998 年からは正式メンバーとなり、G8 が成立する。旧社会主義国ロシアは先進国とはみなされず、「主要 8 か国」と呼ばれた。2014 年、クリミア併合を理由に西側諸国が露主催会合をボイコットし、G7 に戻った。毎年持ち回りの議長国は、2022 年は独。2023 年は日本の広島が開催地。なお、G7 は「先進 7 か国財務相・中央銀行総裁会議」の略称でもある]

◆ (L. 1) **use its influence with 〜** 〜に対する影響力を行使する
◆ (L. 2) **invasion of Ukraine** ウクライナ侵攻(2022 年 2 月、米欧の事前警告を無視して開始された)
◆ (L. 2) **drop "expansive maritime claims" in the South China Sea** 南シナ海における「海洋権益に関する拡張的な主張」を取り下げる(2016 年、オランダ・ハーグの「常設仲裁裁判所」は、「九段線」とそれが囲む南シナ海の領有を主張する中国の「歴史的権利」について、「国際法上の法的根拠がなく、国際法に違反する」と判示したが、中国はこれを無視してきた)
☞◆ (L. 3) **unprecedentedly tough criticism of** 〜への前例を見ないほど強硬な批判 ["unprecedented (ly)" は「前例を見ない(ほどの)」を表す時事英語頻出表現]
☞◆ (L. 3) **Beijing's policies and human rights record** 中国の諸政策及び人権状況("Beijing" の本来の意味は「北京」だが、中国政府を指す。首都名で国名や当該国政府を表す用法。後出の "Moscow" も同様)
◆ (L. 4) **press Russia to pull forces out of Ukraine** ロシアにウクライナから撤兵するよう迫る
◆ (L. 4-5) **immediately and unconditionally** 即時かつ無条件に
◆ (L. 5-6) **a ruling by the International Court of Justice that Moscow suspend its military operation** ロシアが軍事行動を停止すべきとした(国連)国際司法裁判所(ICJ)の判決 [2022 年 3 月、ウクライナの提訴を受け、ICJ はロシアに対しウクライナ侵攻の即時停止を命じた。本来は "…that Moscow should suspend…" となるところ、"rule" など「命令」を含意する動詞に続く "that" 節の "should" は通常省略されるため、"suspend" と原形になっている]
◆ (L. 6) **UN General Assembly resolutions** 国連総会決議(安保理での露の拒否権発動への対応策)
◆ (L. 11) **Chinese foreign ministry spokesman Zhao Lijian** 中国外交部(外務省)趙立堅(ちょうりつけん)報道官(英語発音チャオ・リーチェン)
◆ (L. 11) **a press briefing** 記者説明(報道関係者に対する背景説明、ブリーフィング)
◆ (L. 12) **G7 communique** G7 首脳コミュニケ(共同声明)(コミュニケは仏語の "communiqué" に由来)
◆ (L. 13) **Bavarian Alps** バイエルン・アルプス [独南部の山岳地帯。「ババリア(Bavaria)」は英語。独語では「バイエルン(Bayern)」と呼ぶ。サミット会場のエルマウ城がある]
◆ (L. 14) **the Group of Seven rich industrial democracies** G7 の富裕な工業民主主義国
◆ (L. 14-15) **coercive Chinese non-market policies** 中国の強圧的な非市場主義的政策
◆ (L. 17) **non-transparent and market-distorting interventions** 不透明で市場を歪める政府の介入
◆ (L. 19-20) **the East and South China seas** 東シナ海及び南シナ海
☞◆ (L. 20) **unilateral attempts to change the status quo** 現状を変更しようとする一方的な試み("unilateral" は「一極の」、「一方的な」。派生形の "bilateral"「両極の」、「二国間の」、"multilateral"「多極的な」、「多国間の」などとともに国際関係で多用される表現)
◆ (L. 23-24) **forced labour in Tibet and Xinjiang** チベット及び新疆(しんきょう、英語発音：シンジィアン)ウイグル自治区における強制労働
◆ (L. 24-25) **honour its commitments to uphold rights, freedom and a high degree of autonomy in Hong Kong** 香港における人権、自由及び高度な自治を擁護するとの自ら行った約束を遵守する("honour" は英国綴り)
◆ (L. 26) **NATO summit** NATO サミット(北大西洋条約機構首脳会合)
◆ (L. 28) **growing inclination to flex geopolitical muscle abroad** 地政学的な力を対外的に誇示する傾向が強まっていること

1. 本文の内容と一致するものには T (True) を、一致しないものには F (False) を記せ。

(   ) (1) Group of Seven leaders called for China to exercise its influence with Russia not only to stop its invasion of Ukraine but also abandon its "expansive maritime claims" in the South China Sea.

(   ) (2) China claims that sanctions against Russia will fail to achieve the goal, insisting that the supply of arms to Ukraine by the United States and its allies is far more effective.

(   ) (3) G7 members were "gravely concerned," as stated regularly in previous G7 communiques, about the human rights abuses in China, including forced labour in Tibet and Xinjiang.

(   ) (4) The G7 leaders expressed their serious concern about the situation in the East and South China Seas, opposing any unilateral attempts to change the status quo and increase tensions.

(   ) (5) The G7 communique urges the Chinese government to stick to its commitments to support rights, freedom and a high degree of autonomy in Hong Kong.

2. 次の表は、本文中の ［*Useful Expressions*］ に掲げた表現である "multilateral（多国間)" の首脳会議（サミット）を行う G7 及び G20 を比較したものである。空欄 (1)～(6) に入るべき語を、下記語群 (a)～(h) の中から選んで記号で示せ。大文字、小文字の別はなく、同一番号の空欄は同一語が当てはまるものとする。

	Membership	Scope of Agenda	Chairmanship and Frequency
G7: Group of Seven Leaders Summit (1998～2013 : G8)	• 7 advanced economies	• political issues • (1) issues • economic issues	• by rotation • in (2) order • annually
G20: Group of Twenty "Summit on (3) Markets and the (4) Economy"	• 7 advanced economies • 11 (5) economies • Russian Federation • EU	• (3) issues • economic issues	• by rotation • on a (6) basis • nonregularly

(a) cultural   (b) developed   (c) emerging   (d) financial   (e) prefixed
(f) security   (g) voluntary   (h) world

音声を聞き、下線部を補え。（２回録音されています。１回目はナチュラルスピード、２回目はスロースピードです。）

Natural 22
Slow 24

After all-night talks, members of the World Trade Organization early Friday reached [1] _____ limiting overfishing, broadening production of Covid-19 vaccines in the developing world, improving food security and reforming a 27-year-old trade body that has been back on its heels in recent years. 5

WTO Director-General Nzogi Okonjo-Iweala, after [2] _____ _____, concluded the WTO's first ministerial conference in four and a half years by trumpeting a new sense of cooperation at a time when the world faces crises like Russia's war in Ukraine and a once-in-a-century pandemic that has taken millions of lives. 10

Natural 23
Slow 25

The agreements [3] _____ a trade body that faced repeated criticism from the administration of former U.S. President Donald Trump, which accused the WTO of a lack of fairness to the United States, and that was caught in [4] _____ between the U.S. and China. In recent years, Washington has incapacitated the WTO's 15 version of an appeals court that rules on international trade disputes.

The WTO operates by consensus, meaning that all of its 164 members must agree on its deals—or at least not get in the way. The talks at times took place in backrooms or inside chats because some delegates didn't want to be in the same space as their counterparts from Russia—as a way to protest President Vladimir 20 Putin's invasion of Ukraine, which [5] _____, such as on food and fuel prices.

— Based on an AP report on VOANews.com on June 17, 2022 —

〈ニュース解説〉　コロナの世界的蔓延やロシアのウクライナ侵攻などにより、世界貿易を巡る課題が山積する中、世界貿易機関の閣僚会議が４年半ぶりにジュネーブの本部で開催された。徹夜交渉の結果、魚類の乱獲防止やコロナワクチン増産等のほか、設立四半世紀を迎えた WTO の運営に関する改革についても一定の合意がなされた。

(Notes)
World Trade Organization 世界貿易機関　**overfishing** 魚類の乱獲　**developing world** 開発途上地域　**food security** 食糧安全保障　**a 27-year-old trade body**（1995 年に設立された WTO を指す）　**back on its heels** 低迷している　**Director-General Nzogi Okonjo-Iweala** ゴズィ・オコンジョ＝イウェアラ事務局長（ナイジェリアの政治家）　**ministerial conference** 閣僚会議　**a once-in-a-century pandemic** 100 年に一度のパンデミック（世界的感染爆発）　**former U.S. President Donald Trump** ドナルド・トランプ前米大統領　**the WTO's version of an appeals court** WTO 上級委員会（WTO 版上訴裁判所）（正式名称 "Appellate Body"）　**rule on international trade disputes** 国際貿易紛争に裁定を下す　**by consensus** 全会一致で　**not get in the way** 異議を唱えない（邪魔をしない）　**backrooms**（議場外の）別室　**inside chats** 小グループ内のチャット　**delegates**（加盟メンバーの）代表団　**counterparts**（対等の立場にあるもの。ここでは "delegates" を指す）　**President Vladimir Putin** ウラジーミル・プーチン露大統領

■問A　空所 (a) 〜 (f) にそれぞれ入るべき 1 語を下記の語群から選びその番号を記せ。

国連総会（UNGA）	→	United Nations General (a)
国連安全保障理事会（UNSC）	→	United Nations Security (b)
国連難民高等弁務官（UNHCR）	→	United Nations High (c) for Refugees
国連食糧農業機関（FAO）	→	(United Nations) Food and Agriculture (d)
国際原子力機関（IAEA）	→	International Atomic Energy (e)
国際通貨基金（IMF）	→	International Monetary (f)

| 1. Agency | 2. Assembly | 3. Commissioner | 4. Council |
| 5. Forum | 6. Fund | 7. Operation | 8. Organization |

■問B　(a) 〜 (k) にそれぞれ入るべき 1 語を下記の語群から選びその番号を記せ。

国連教育科学文化機関（UNESCO）	→	United Nations (a), Scientific and Cultural Organization
国際労働機関（ILO）	→	International (b) Organization
世界保健機関（WHO）	→	World (c) Organization
世界貿易機関（WTO）	→	World (d) Organization
国際復興開発銀行（IBRD）	→	International Bank for (e) and Development
アジア太平洋経済協力（APEC）	→	Asia-Pacific (f) Cooperation
東南アジア諸国連合（ASEAN）	→	(g) of Southeast Asian Nations
北大西洋条約機構（NATO）	→	North Atlantic (h) Organization
石油輸出国機構（OPEC）	→	Organization of the (i) Exporting Countries
経済協力開発機構（OECD）	→	Organisation for Economic (j) and Development
国際エネルギー機関（IEA）	→	International (k) Agency

1. Association	2. Co-operation	3. Countries	4. Economic
5. Educational	6. Energy	7. Healing	8. Health
9. Labour	10. Leaders	11. Petroleum	12. Power
13. Reconstruction	14. Rehabilitation	15. Trade	16. Treaty

■問C　(a) 〜 (g) をそれぞれ和訳せよ。

(a) Ambassador Extraordinary and Plenipotentiary
(b) diplomatic immunity
(c) ratification
(d) sovereignty
(e) COP
(f) exile
(g) economic sanctions

The lead — リードの役割

すべてのニュースがこの形をとるわけではないが、特に "hard news" は、リードと呼ばれる導入部でニュースの要約を伝えるのが普通である。一般に five W's and one H のすべての要素が、最初の1〜2の段落に凝縮される。「lead（リード）」は「headline（見出し）」のすぐ後に書かれ、リードの後に続くのが「body（本文）」である。ヘッドラインはスペース上の問題もあり記事の内容を正確に伝えきれないこともあるが、リードは記事の内容を冒頭で要約して、読者に端的に伝える。

このトピックを英文で読んでみよう。

A news story has two main parts: a lead and a body.

Usually the lead is the opening paragraph but may include the second and third paragraphs as well. It is the essence of the news as presented in summary form at the beginning of the story.

A typical lead is:

Telephone wires leading into 15 dwellings were cut yesterday afternoon, apparently by vandals, interrupting service for 25 users.

Leads have many constructions and patterns of their own. Generally, however, they seek to answer six questions about the news—Who? What? When? Where? Why? and How?

The body of the story is all the rest beyond the lead, no matter whether the remainder is three or 30 paragraphs long. The arrangement of the body often follows logically from the lead, but it, too, must be planned.

Suspect, Charged, Said to Admit to Role in Plot

By Mark Mazzetti, Sabrina Tavernise And Jack Healy

Lead

A Pakistani-American man arrested in the failed Times Square car bombing has admitted his role in the attempted attack and said he received explosives training in Pakistan, the authorities said Tuesday.

The man, Faisal Shahzad, 30, was arrested as he tried to flee the country in a Dubai-bound jet late Monday. Hours later, there were reports that seven or eight people had been arrested in Pakistan, as officials in both countries sought to

FBI search a house where Faisal Shahzad lived in Bridgeport, Conn., Tuesday, May 4, 2010.

confirmed, it would be the group's first effort to attack the United States and the first sign of the

booked a ticket on his way to Kennedy Airport and bought it with cash when he got there. officials

Officials said Mr. Shahzad had been placed on a no-fly list on Monday afternoon, but they declined to explain how he had been allowed to board the plane. An Isuzu Trooper that Mr. Shahzad had apparently driven to the airport was found in a parking lot. Inside the Trooper, investigators discovered a Kel-Tec 9-millimeter pistol, with a folding stock and a rifle barrel, along with several spare magazines of ammunition, an official said. Fearing the Izuzu might be rigged to explode, officials briefly cordoned off the area around it. All of the passengers were taken off the plane, and they, their luggage and the Boeing 777 were screened

before the flight w depart, about seven 6:29 a.m. Two other interviewed by the released, according enforcement officia said Mr. Shahza providing "useful i federal investigator pulled off the plane. that he had receiv Pakistan, Mr. Shah acted alone, a clain being investigated. In Pakistan, unfolded quickl Tauhid Ahmed an been in touch with through e-mail and

NEWS 5

Russia's Lavrov says Moscow wants more territory; US sees grinding war

Russian Foreign Minister Sergey Lavrov said Wednesday that Moscow wants to capture territory in southern Ukraine beyond the eastern Donbas region as the US and its allies committed more military aid to Ukraine.

Russia failed in the early stages of its five-month offensive to topple the government of Ukrainian President Volodymyr Zelenskyy or capture the capital, 5 Kyiv, in northern Ukraine. And it is currently battling Ukrainian forces for control of the Donbas region.

But Lavrov said in an interview Wednesday with state media that Russia no longer feels constrained to fighting in the Donbas where Russian separatists have been battling Kyiv's forces since 2014 when Russia seized Ukraine's Crimean 10 Peninsula. "Now, the geography has changed. It's not just Donetsk and Luhansk. It's Kherson, Zaporizhia and several other territories." Lavrov told the state news RT television and RIA Novosti news agency.

27 Lavrov, Russia's top diplomat, said Moscow's territorial objectives would expand still further if Western countries delivered more long-range missiles to Kyiv. 15 The US announced Wednesday plans to send four more such rocket systems to Ukraine, along with more artillery rounds.

"Ukrainian forces are now using long-range rocket systems to great effect, including HIMARS provided by the United States, and other systems from our allies and partners," US Defense Secretary Lloyd Austin said Wednesday at the Pentagon. 20 "Ukraine's defenders are pushing hard to hold Russia's advances in the Donbas."

General Mark Milley, chairman of the Joint Chiefs of Staff, said the Ukrainians have been using US-supplied multiple rocket launchers to hit Russian command centers and supply lines, including a strategically important bridge across the Dnieper River in the Kherson region. 25

Russian officials said the bridge has sustained damage but is still open to some traffic. The Russian military would be hard-pressed to keep supplying its forces in the region if the bridge were destroyed. "The Ukrainians are making the Russians pay for every inch of territory that they gain," Milley said, and the Donbas is "not lost yet. The Ukrainians intend to continue the fight." 30

— *Based on a report on VOANews.com on July 20, 2022* —

〈ニュース解説〉　ロシアのウクライナ侵攻は世界に衝撃を与えた。ロシアは 2014 年にクリミアを併合して以後、ウクライナ東部地域のドネツク州とルハンスク州で親ロシア派勢力を支援し、親ロシア派によるウクライナからの独立を一方的に承認していた。ロシアの軍事侵攻はその直後に起こり、上記 2 州の他に、首都キーウやウクライナ第 2 の都市ハリキウへの攻撃を開始した。現在戦況は膠着状態とも言え、短期での決着を予想していたプーチン政権には大誤算となった。ロシアは、東部 2 州の制圧だけでなく、ヘルソン州等の南部地域の制圧を狙うが、ウクライナ軍の反攻に会っている。

(Notes)　【※☞マークは *Useful Expressions*】

◆　**Lavrov**　セルゲイ・ラブロフ（Sergey Lavrov。ロシアの外務大臣）

◆　(L. 2)　**Donbas region**　ドンバス地方（ウクライナ南東部の地方。ドネツク州とルハンスク州を含む）

◆　(L. 5)　**Volodymyr Zelenskyy**　ウォロディミル・ゼレンスキー（ウクライナ第 6 代大統領。元俳優・コメディアン）

◆　(L. 6)　**Kyiv**　キーウ（ウクライナの首都。「キーウ」はウクライナ語由来。ロシアのウクライナ侵攻前までは、我が国でもロシア語のキエフの呼称が使われていた）

◆　(L. 9)　**Russian separatists**　ロシア分離主義者（親ロシアの分離武装勢力のことで、ロシアからの直接、間接の支援を受け、ロシア系住民だけでなくロシア軍から送り込まれた兵員がいるとも言われる）

◆　(L. 10-11)　**Crimean Peninsula**　クリミア半島（ウクライナ南部、黒海北岸にある半島。2014 年に半島全域をロシアが編入。ウクライナ政府や国際社会の多くはこれを認めていない）

◆　(L. 12)　**Kherson**　ヘルソン州（ウクライナ南部、クリミア半島の北に位置する州。州都はドニエプル川が流れるヘルソン。2022 年のロシアのウクライナ軍事侵攻で、ロシアは州の全域を制圧したと発表し、同州のロシア化を進めようとしている）

◆　(L. 12)　**Zaporizhia**　ザポリージャ州（ウクライナ南東部にある州。ドネツク州とヘルソン州の間に位置する。州都はザポリージャ。ロシア軍の砲撃で一部施設が火災を起こした欧州最大のザポリージャ原子力発電所がある）

◆　(L. 12-13)　**RT television**　ロシア・トゥデイ（Russia Today。モスクワのニュース専門局。西側諸国からは、ロシア政府のプロパガンダ局とみなされ、フェイクニュースの拡散を行っているとの批判がある）

◆　(L. 13)　**RIA Novosti news agency**　リア・ノーボスチ通信社（かつてのロシア国営通信社。ノーボスチはロシア語でニュースの意）

☞◆　(L. 17)　**along with**　〜と一緒に、〜と共に

◆　(L. 17)　**artillery rounds**　砲弾

☞◆　(L. 18)　**use 〜 to great effect**　〜を使って大きな成果をあげる。最大限に用いる

◆　(L. 19)　**HIMARS**　ハイマース、高機動ロケット砲システム［High Mobility Artillery Rocket System の略。米国陸軍が開発した自走多連装のロケット砲である。従来の多連装ロケットシステム MLRS（Multiple Launch Rocket System）と比べ、小型軽量化されている］

◆　(L. 20)　**Lloyd Austin**　ロイド・オースティン（米国国防長官。2021 年 1 月、アフリカ系米国人初の国防長官に就任）

◆　(L. 20)　**Pentagon**　ペンタゴン、米国防総省（国防総省の建物が 5 角形であるためにこの通称がある。正式英語名称は "Department of Defense"。日本語名は、陸海空の各省を統括していることから、「国防省」ではなく「国防総省」）

◆　(L. 22)　**General Mark Milley, chairman of the Joint Chiefs of Staff**　マーク・ミリー統合参謀本部議長（米陸軍大将。ミリーが 2019 年に就任した統合参謀本部議長は、米軍を統率する軍人のトップ）

◆　(L. 23)　**multiple rocket launchers**　多連装ロケット砲

◆　(L. 24-25)　**Dnieper River**　ドニエプル川（ロシア、ベラルーシを経て、ウクライナのキーウ、ザポリージャ、ヘルソンから黒海に流れ込む全長 2285 キロの大河）

◆　(L. 27)　**hard-pressed**　苦境に立たされて

1. 本文の内容と一致するものには T (True) を、一致しないものには F (False) を記せ。

(　) (1) Russia's foreign minister is ready to propose a ceasefire as the war is not going in their favor.

(　) (2) The Russians expected a speedy victory over Ukrainian forces, but that has not been materialized yet.

(　) (3) The Ukrainian president is ready to give up the Donbas region if the Russians promise not to take the Ukrainian capital.

(　) (4) It can easily be verified that Sergey Lavrov and Volodymyr Zelenskyy are on good terms with each other.

(　) (5) It can be assumed that Russia's territorial ambitions of expanding further into the southern Ukrainian regions were instigated by the delivery of long-range missiles to Ukraine by Western nations.

(　) (6) Long-range rocket systems like HIMARS, provided by the United States and its allies, seem to be achieving their intended tactical results.

(　) (7) Ukrainian troops were reluctant to destroy a bridge over the Dnieper River in consideration of recovery and restoration efforts after the possible ceasefire.

(　) (8) The chairman of the US Joint Chiefs of Staff maintains a positive look at the current situation in Ukraine where Ukrainian forces are fighting hard trying to halt Russian advances.

2. 本文中に掲げた下記の [*Useful Expressions*] を用いて空欄に適語を記し、日本語に合う英文を完成させよ。

(1) 〈**along with**〉

I usually spend half an hour (　　　　　　　　　　　　　　　　　).

私は朝食とともにコーヒーを 30 分かけてちびちび飲むことを常としている。

(2) 〈**use 〜 to great effect**〉

The lawyer used (　　　　　　　　　　　) in influencing the judge's decision.

その弁護士は、自身の法律知識を最大限使って裁判官の判決に影響を及ぼした。

音声を聞き、下線部を補え。（２回録音されています。１回目はナ
チュラルスピード、２回目はスロースピードです。）

Natural 28
Slow 30

China's Foreign Minister Wang Yi on Monday urged the Pacific region not to be "too anxious" about his country's aims after a meeting in Fiji with his counterparts from 10 island nations was unable to agree to [(1)](_____
_____).

Wang hosted the meeting with foreign ministers from Pacific island nations with diplomatic ties with China midway through a diplomatic tour of the region where Beijing's ambitions for wider security ties [(2)](_____
_____).

A draft communique and five-year action plan sent by China to the invited nations ahead of the meeting showed China was seeking a sweeping regional trade and security agreement.

Natural 29
Slow 31

But the draft communique prompted opposition [(3)](_____
_____), Federated States of Micronesia, according to a letter leaked last week.

After the meeting, which included Samoa, Tonga, Kiribati, Papua New Guinea, Solomon Islands, Niue and Vanuatu, Wang said the nations had agreed on five areas of cooperation, but [(4)](_____) to shape more consensus.

The five areas he listed included economic recovery after the Covid pandemic, and new centers for agriculture and disaster, but did not include security. The United States, Australia, Japan and New Zealand have expressed concern about a security pact signed by the Solomon Islands with China last month, saying it had regional consequences and [(5)](_____) close to Australia.

— Based on a report on CNN.com on May 30, 2022 —

5

10

15

20

〈ニュース解説〉　西太平洋から米軍の影響力を排除したい中国は、ミクロネシア、メラネシア、ポリネシアの太平洋諸島各国との経済、安全保障分野での協定締結に向け王毅外相を派遣した。既にソロモン諸島が中国と締結した安全保障協定の内容が漏れ、日、米、豪、ニュージーランドは、中国によるソロモン諸島軍事拠点化に繋がるのではないかと警戒する。ソロモン諸島の首都ホニアラは、太平洋戦争の激戦地ガダルカナル島にあり、今回の中国の動きは、当時米豪間の連絡路にくさびを打ち込もうとした旧日本軍の戦略を彷彿させる。

(Notes)
China's Foreign Minister Wang Yi 王毅中国外務大臣（正式な肩書は「外交部長」）　**Fiji** フィジー共和国（首都はスバ）　**Federated States of Micronesia** ミクロネシア連邦（嘗て日本の委任統治、米国の信託統治の期間があり、両国との関係は深い。日系２世、４世が大統領に就いたこともあった）　**Samoa** サモア（首都アピア。ポリネシア系文化を維持）　**Tonga** トンガ（ポリネシアにある立憲君主国。2022年１月の海底火山の大噴火で大きな被害を受けた）　**Kiribati** キリバス共和国（地球温暖化による海面上昇で国土の半分以上が水没する危機を訴えてきた。近年やや中国寄りの政策が目立つ）　**Papua New Guinea** パプアニューギニア（ニューギニア島の東半分と周辺島嶼部からなる立憲君主国。中国から多額の借款を受けている）　**Solomon Islands** ソロモン諸島（2019年台湾と断交。マナセ・ソガバレ首相のもとで中国との関係強化）　**Niue** ニウエ（トンガの東に位置する立憲君主国。ニュージーランドとの関係が深い）　**Vanuatu** バヌアツ共和国

■問A 自衛隊関連用語 (a) ～ (d) にそれぞれ入るべき 1 語を下記の語群から選びその番号を記せ。

自衛隊　　　　→　Japan Self-Defense (a)
陸上自衛隊　　→　Japan (b) Self-Defense Force
海上自衛隊　　→　Japan (c) Self-Defense Force
航空自衛隊　　→　Japan (d) Self-Defense Force

> 1. Air　　2. Force　　3. Forces　　4. Ground　　5. Maritime　　6. Sea

■問B 米軍関連用語 (a) ～ (e) をそれぞれ和訳せよ。

(a) United States Armed Forces
(b) United States Army
(c) United States Navy
(d) United States Air Force
(e) United States Marine Corps

■問C 軍事用語 (a) ～ (d) をそれぞれ和訳せよ。

(a) anti-ballistic missile (ABM)
(b) airborne warning and control system (AWACS)
(c) intermediate-range ballistic missile (IRBM)［射程距離の短い準中距離弾道ミサイルは、medium-range ballistic missile（MRBM）と呼ばれるが、IRBM との区別は明確ではない］
(d) Nuclear Non-Proliferation Treaty (NPT)

■問D (a) ～ (j) にそれぞれ対応する英語表現を下記の語群から選びその番号を記せ。

(a) 平和維持活動　　(b) 非武装地帯　　(c) 文民統制　　(d) 核軍縮
(e) 核保有国　　(f) 通常兵器　　(g) 地雷　　(h) 休戦
(i) 大量破壊兵器　　(j) 自爆テロ

> 1. ceasefire　　　　　　　　2. civilian control
> 3. conventional weapons　　4. demilitarized zone (DMZ)
> 5. landmine　　　　　　　　6. nuclear disarmament
> 7. nuclear powers　　　　　8. peacekeeping operations
> 9. terrorist suicide bombing　10. weapons of mass destruction (WMD)

Beyond the basic news lead ― 異なるスタイルのリード

社会問題や面白そうな人物を扱った記事等、解説的要素が大きく入り込む記事においては、前章で触れたような事実だけを並べた要約的なリードで記事を書き始めたのでは何とも味気ない。すべてのニュースが時宜を得たものであるとは限らない。昨日今日のニュースのように即時性が要求されるニュースでない場合は、もっと生き生きしたクリエイティヴで掘り下げた、場合によっては楽しく人をわくわくさせる記事の書き方が求められる。

このトピックを英文で読んでみよう。

It is not mandatory to begin every story with a roundup of essential facts. For most breaking news events, you need leads that are quick, factual, and concise. You need leads that summarize the who-what-when-where-why. But not every story is a timely news event. Some stories explore social issues. Some profile interesting people. And for those, a basic news lead may be too dull and dry. You may need something livelier, snappier, more creative, a lead that does not just summarize, but amuses, astonishes, and intrigues.

NEWS MEDIA IN THE WORLD

通信社　News Agencies (1)

✔ "news agency" や "news service" と呼ばれる「通信社」は、独自の取材陣又は国内外の報道機関などと連携し、作成したニュース記事を写真やビデオ映像などとともに新聞社、放送会社へ配信する組織。膨大な取材ネットワークが必要なため、単独の新聞社等では対応が困難なことから、報道機関が共同して通信社を設ける非営利型の組合組織も多い。

NEWS 6

Disk 1
(32)

Boris Johnson quits as UK prime minister, dragged down by scandals

Scandal-ridden Boris Johnson announced on Thursday he would quit as British prime minister after he dramatically lost the support of his ministers and most Conservative lawmakers, but said he would stay on until his successor was chosen.

Bowing to the inevitable as more than 50 government ministers and aides quit and lawmakers said he must go, an isolated and powerless Johnson said it was clear 5 his party wanted someone else in charge, but that his forced departure was "eccentric" and the result of "herd instinct" in parliament.

"Today I have appointed a cabinet to serve, as I will, until a new leader is in place," Johnson said outside his Downing Street office where his speech was watched by close allies and his wife Carrie. "I know that there will be many people who are 10 relieved and perhaps quite a few who will also be disappointed. And I want you to know how sad I am to be giving up the best job in the world. But them's the breaks," he added, making no apology for the events that forced his announcement.

His term in office was ended by scandals that included breaches of Covid-19 pandemic lockdown rules, a luxury renovation of his official residence and the 15 appointment of a minister who had been accused of sexual misconduct.

There were cheers and applause as he began his speech, while boos rang out (33) from some outside the gates of Downing Street.

After days of battling for his job, Johnson had been deserted by all but a handful of his closest allies after the latest in a series of scandals sapped their willingness to 20 support him. The Conservatives will now have to elect a new leader, a process which could take weeks or months, with details to be announced next week.

Johnson is leaving behind an economy in crisis. Britons are facing the tightest squeeze on their finances in decades in the wake of the pandemic, with soaring inflation. The economy is forecast to be the weakest among major nations in 2023 25 apart from Russia.

The ebullient Johnson came to power nearly three years ago, promising to deliver Brexit and rescue it from the bitter wrangling that followed the 2016 referendum. He shrugged off concerns from some that his narcissism, failure to deal with details, and a reputation for deceit meant he was unsuitable. 30

— Based on a report on Reuters.com on July 8, 2022 —

〈ニュース解説〉　ボリス・ジョンソン英国首相が、2022年7月7日、度重なるスキャンダルと閣僚の大量辞任の責任を取り、辞意を表明した。2019年7月、英国の「欧州離脱（Brexit ブレグジット）」の実施期限が迫る中、与野党からの信任を失い辞任したテリーザ・メイ氏の後任首相に就任。Brexit実現等の業績を上げたが、ワンマンな政治姿勢等で物議をかもした。ジョンソン氏の辞任表明は、日英関係強化の盟友だった安倍元首相が凶弾に倒れる数時間前のことだった。後任の新政権は景気減速による税収減とインフレ対策という困難な財政運営を迫られることとなる。

(Notes)　【※☞マークは *Useful Expressions*】

◆ **Boris Johnson quits as UK prime minister, dragged down by scandals**　「ボリス・ジョンソン英国首相辞任　スキャンダルの責任取る」〔"Boris Johnson" ボリス・ジョンソン氏は米国生まれ。イートン校、オックスフォード大学を経て、保守的な英紙デイリー・テレグラフの記者となり、EU（欧州連合）に批判的な記事を書く。政界入り後、下院議員、ロンドン市長を経て、メイ政権の外相となったが、穏健な離脱案に反対して辞任。後任外相のジェレミー・ハント氏との保守党党首選の決戦投票を制し、2019年7月、第77代英国首相となった。特徴のある容姿、過激な言動により保守党の異端児とされてきたが、国民的な人気があり、親しみを持って「ボリス」と呼ばれる。親米派。首相就任後は、巧みな行動力と駆け引きでEUとの困難な交渉をまとめ、ブレグジットを実現した。この間、安倍元首相とも親交を深め、日英関係の強化や「自由で開かれたインド太平洋」の確立に貢献した。"UK" は "United Kingdom（連合王国）" の略称で「英国」を指す一般的な用語〕

☞◆ **(L. 1)　scandal-ridden**　スキャンダルに悩まされて来た（"ridden" は "ride" の過去分詞 "-ridden" の形で「〜に支配された」、「〜でがんじがらめになった」という合成語を作る）

◆ **(L. 3)　Conservative lawmakers**　保守党議会議員（後出の "the Conservatives" は集合的に「保守党」を表す。1832年旧「トーリー党」から改称したが、"the Tories" は保守党のあだ名として現在でも使われている）

◆ **(L. 3)　stay on until his successor was chosen**　後任決定まで、首相職に留まる〔9月6日、保守党党首選を制したリズ・トラス（Liz Truss）外務大臣が、英国三人目の女性首相に就任した〕

◆ **(L. 4)　bowing to the inevitable**　避けられない運命に屈服して

◆ **(L. 6)　eccentric**　常軌を逸した、風変わりな、奇矯な

◆ **(L. 7)　herd instinct**　群居本能（すぐに群れたがる習性。短時日に50人以上となる閣僚等の辞任連鎖が起きたことは、議会における同調圧力の結果ではないかとの含意がある）

◆ **(L. 9)　Downing Street office**　首相官邸〔"Downing Street" は首相官邸が所在する小路。特に官邸の所在番地である「ダウニング街10番地（the Downing 10）」は首相官邸の代名詞。11番地は財務相（Chancellor of the Exchequer）官邸〕

◆ **(L. 10)　close allies and his wife Carrie**　ジョンソン氏の親密な協力者とキャリー夫人

◆ **(L. 12)　them's the breaks**　まあ仕方ない、これも宿命だ（口語表現。"them's" は "those are" の短縮形）

◆ **(L. 14-15)　breaches of COVID-19 pandemic lockdown rules**　コロナ・パンデミックのロックダウン規則違反（2020年11月のロックダウン期間中に官邸でパーティーを開いたことが批判された）

◆ **(L. 15)　a luxury renovation of his official residence**　首相官邸の豪華なリノベーション（改装）

◆ **(L. 16)　had been accused of sexual misconduct**　性的不品行で告発されていた

◆ **(L. 17)　cheers and applause**　歓声と拍手

◆ **(L. 17)　boos rang out**　ブーイングが鳴り響いた

◆ **(L. 23)　is leaving behind an economy in crisis**　危機的状況にある経済を残すことになる（☞ "leave behind 〜「〜を後に残す」）

◆ **(L. 23)　Britons**　英国人（"the British" と同義だが、主に新聞報道で使われる文語的表現）

◆ **(L. 23-24)　tightest squeeze on their finances**　最も厳しい財政状況（"squeeze" は「（経済的）困窮」の意）

◆ **(L. 24-25)　soaring inflation**　インフレーションの急激な亢進

◆ **(L. 28)　deliver Brexit and rescue it from the bitter wrangling**　ブレグジット（英国の欧州離脱）を実現し、激しい論争に終止符を打つ

◆ **(L. 28-29)　the 2016 referendum**　（欧州連合からの離脱の是非を問う）2016年の国民投票

◆ **(L. 29)　narcissism**　自己中心的（ナルシシズム）

◆ **(L. 30)　a reputation for deceit**　欺瞞的だとの評判

1. 本文の内容と一致するものには T (True) を、一致しないものには F (False) を記せ。

(　　　) (1) Taking responsibility for series of scandals, UK Prime Minister Boris Johnson announced his resignation, and said he would not stay in office even before his successor was chosen.

(　　　) (2) Johnson decided to resign, realising it was inevitable when more than 50 ministers and aides left the government and lawmakers said he must go.

(　　　) (3) In his speech in front of the Downing Street office, Mr Johnson made an apology for the events that forced his announcement of resignation.

(　　　) (4) With the announcement of Johnson's resignation, the Conservative Party would have to elect a new leader.

(　　　) (5) The British economy is in a crisis caused by the pandemic and skyrocketing inflation and is projected to be the weakest among major powers in 2023, including Russia.

(　　　) (6) Despite concerns about his personality, way of thinking and working style, Boris Johnson came to power, pledging to fulfil Brexit.

2. 本文中に掲げた［*Useful Expressions*］を参照し、下記の語群を並び替えて空欄に適語を記し、日本語に合う英文を完成させよ。

(1) 過剰な負債を抱えたその会社は、自己破産を選ぶほか道はなかった。

The debt-(　　　) (　　　) (　　　) (　　　) (　　　) (　　　) to declare voluntary bankruptcy.

> but,　choice,　company,　had,　no,　ridden

(2) 日本の平安時代は偉大な文化遺産を残した。

Japan's Heian period (　　　) (　　　) (　　　) (　　　) (　　　) heritage.

> a,　behind,　cultural,　great,　left

音声を聞き、下線部を補え。（２回録音されています。１回目はナチュラルスピード、２回目はスロースピードです。）

Natural
34
Slow
36

The House sent President Joe Biden (1)
Congress has passed in decades on Friday, a measured compromise that at once illustrates progress on the long-intractable issue and the deep-seated partisan divide that persists.

The Democratic-led chamber approved the election-year legislation on a mostly party-line 234-193 vote, (2) _____ voters' revulsion over last month's mass shootings in Buffalo, New York, and Uvalde, Texas. The night before, the Senate approved it by a bipartisan 65-33 margin, with 15 Republicans joining all Democrats in supporting a package that senators from both parties had crafted.

Natural
35
Slow
37

The bill would incrementally (3) _____,
deny firearms to more domestic abusers, and help local authorities temporarily take weapons from people judged to be dangerous. Most of its $13 billion cost would go to bolster mental health programs for schools that have been targeted in Newtown, Connecticut, Parkland, Florida, and many other mass shootings.

And while it omits the far tougher restrictions Democrats have long championed, it stands (4) _____ that Congress has approved since it enacted a now-expired assault weapons ban nearly 30 years ago.

For the conservatives who dominate Republicans in the House, it all came down to the Constitution's Second Amendment right for people to have firearms, a protection that is (5) _____.

— *Based on an AP report on VOANews.com on June 24, 2022* —

5

10

15

20

〈ニュース解説〉　人口を上回る約3億丁もの銃があるとされる米国。学校等での銃乱射事件が後を絶たず、その規制は国論を分断する困難な課題となってきた。規制に前向きなバイデン政権だが、一方の保守派は、合衆国憲法修正第2条に規定される「人民の武装権」を根拠に慎重な姿勢を崩さない。今回、上下両院では民主、共和両党の妥協により、銃所持の許可条件強化や銃撃事件のメンタルケアへの支出を含む広範な規制法が成立した。この問題は、中絶禁止の在り方等とともに2022年11月の中間選挙の争点になりそうだ。（CH8 EX2の関連記事参照）

(Notes)

The House 米国下院（"House of Representatives" の略称）　**President Joe Biden** ジョー・バイデン米大統領　**Congress** 米議会　**measured compromise** 慎重に見出された妥協案　**long-intractable issue** 長きにわたる困難な課題　**deep-seated partisan divide** 根強い党派的分断　**Democratic-led chamber** 民主党が多数を占める下院　**election-year legislation** （2年ごとの）選挙実施年における立法案　**on a mostly party-line vote** ほぼ党の方針に沿った投票〔自党に反対又は反対党に賛成することを「交差投票（cross-voting）」と呼ぶ〕　**mass shootings** 大規模銃撃事件　**Buffalo, New York and Uvalde, Texas** ニューヨーク州バッファロー、テキサス州ユバルディ（いずれも大規模銃撃事件があった）　**the Senate** （米国）上院（後出 "senator" は上院議員）　**by a bipartisan 65-33 margin** 65対33となる超党派（の賛成）で　**Republicans** 共和党（共和党員の複数形で集合的に共和党を指す。後出 "Democrats" は民主党）　**a package** 修正を加えた合意案　**domestic abusers** DV（家庭内暴力の）加害者　**local authorities** 地域警察当局　**go to bolster mental health programs** メンタル・ヘルス・プログラム強化のために使われる　**Newtown, Connecticut, Parkland, Florida** コネチカット州ニュータウン、フロリダ州パークランド（ともに学校内での銃乱射事件があった）　**have long championed** 長い間（法案の）擁護者となって支持してきた　**a now-expired assault weapons ban** 現在期限切れとなっているアサルト・ウェポン（銃器）禁止法　**conservatives who dominate Republicans** 共和党を支配する保守派　**the Constitution's Second Amendment** 合衆国憲法修正第2条　**right for people to have firearms** 人民が銃器を所有する権利

■問A 米国政府関連用語 (a) 〜 (i) にそれぞれ入るべき 1 語を下記の語群から選びその番号を記せ。

司法省　　　　　　　→　Department of (a)
財務省　　　　　　　→　Department of the (b)
内務省　　　　　　　→　Department of the (c)
国防総省　　　　　　→　Department of (d)
中央情報局　　　　　→　Central (e) Agency
国家安全保障会議　　→　National (f) Council
連邦捜査局　　　　　→　Federal Bureau of (g)
米国通商代表部　　　→　Office of the United States (h) Representative
国土安全保障省　　　→　Department of (i) Security

> 1. Defense　2. Homeland　3. Intelligence　4. Interior　5. Investigation
> 6. Justice　7. Security　8. Trade　9. Treasury

■問B (a) 〜 (o) にそれぞれ対応する英文名称を下記の語群から選びその番号を記せ。

(a)（米）連邦議会　　　(b)（米）下院　　　　(c)（米）上院
(d)（英）議会　　　　　(e)（英）下院　　　　(f)（英）上院
(g)（米）民主党　　　　(h)（米）共和党　　　(i)（英）自由民主党
(j)（英）労働党　　　　(k)（英）保守党　　　(l)（米）国務長官
(m)（米）司法長官　　　(n)（英）内相　　　　(o)（英）財務相（蔵相）

> 1. Attorney General　　　　　　2. Chancellor of the Exchequer
> 3. Congress　　　　　　　　　　4. Conservative Party
> 5. Democratic Party　　　　　　6. Home Secretary
> 7. House of Commons　　　　　　8. House of Lords
> 9. House of Representatives　　10. Labour Party
> 11. Liberal Democratic Party　12. Parliament
> 13. Republican Party　　　　　 14. Secretary of State
> 15. Senate

■問C (a) 〜 (e) のアジア関連用語をそれぞれ和訳せよ。

(a) National People's Congress
(b) People's Liberation Army
(c) People's Daily
(d) Republic of Korea (ROK)
(e) Democratic People's Republic of Korea (DPRK)

The world of features — フィーチャー・ニュースの世界

"feature news"（フィーチャー・ニュース）は日本語では「特集記事」や「読み物」などと訳される。また、"hard news" と対比して "soft news" と呼ばれることもある。日本を台風が直撃し、その当日あるいは翌日、その被害を報じれば "hard news" である。その後、台風で家を失った住民の生活に焦点を当てて報じれば "feature news" となる。新聞などで報じられるニュースの大半は "hard news" であるが、報道のスピードという点で新聞はインターネットに遅れを取らざるを得ず、インターネットの普及に伴い、新聞の記事に占める "feature news" の割合が増加傾向にあるとの指摘もある。

このトピックを英文で読んでみよう。

Some old-timers treat news and features as if they are two separate things. News, they insist, is the factual reporting of serious events, while features involve all that other, nonessential stuff. It is not that simple, though. Journalists often find it difficult to distinguish between news and features. News stories usually focus on events that are timely and public: government activity, crime, disasters. Feature stories often focus on issues that are less timely and more personal: trends, relationships, entertainment. News stories tell you what happened; feature stories offer you advice, explore ideas, and make you laugh and cry.

NEWS MEDIA IN THE WORLD

通信社　News Agencies (2)

✓　世界最初の近代的通信社は 1835 年フランスに生まれたアバスを母体とする AFP 通信（Agence France-Presse）。19 世紀半ばに創立の英国のロイター通信（Reuters）も業界の老舗。同時期に米国で設立された AP 通信（Associated Press）は組合型通信社の最大手。両社とも全世界に取材網を持ち、近時は経済ニュースにも力を入れる。経済情報の分野では Bloomberg の影響力も侮れない。

NEWS 7

Disk 1
38

Tokyo senior highs to retire rules that forced conformity

Strict rules that governed Tokyo high school students from the color and style of their hair to the color of their underwear will soon be a relic of the rigid past.

Tokyo metropolitan senior high schools have announced they will do away with five rules long considered irrational that mandated conformity in the classroom.

"The times have changed and this is now likely a time to convert to a new way 5 of guiding students," one education board member said about the rules elimination. "While it may take time, we want to continue deciding on rules while holding discussions with students."

The rules included one requiring all students to have their hair black and banning undercut hair styles that have the hair longer on top and buzzed on the sides. 10

The rule designating the color of underwear to be worn to school will also go out the window as well as the rather ambiguous one about teachers guiding their pupils to act as proper senior high school students.

The disciplinary measure of forcing problem students to remain at home will also be retired. 15

The rules will be eliminated from the school year starting in April. The decision is based on discussions held at each Tokyo metropolitan senior high school involving students, teachers and parents.

39 One male student who will enter his third year of high school in April said, "This issue has gained this much attention because so many students have found the rules 20 discomforting. It is only natural to do away with those rules."

Between March and April 2021, the Tokyo metropolitan board of education asked all schools to review the five rules along with a sixth asking students to voluntarily submit forms certifying the natural color of their hair or that they had natural wavy hair. 25

Of the 240 programs available at the 196 metropolitan senior high schools, 216 programs included some of those rules.

The rule about natural hair color and wave will be eliminated at 35 of the 55 programs that had it, but remain in place at the other 20 programs.

The students asked that the rule about natural hair color and wave remain on 30 the grounds that informing the school about the color and wave would do away with needless instructions from teachers about their hair.

The issue first gained national attention in 2017 when a female student at an Osaka prefectural senior high school filed a lawsuit seeking compensation from the education board for the emotional distress she endured from teachers who repeatedly 35 asked her to dye her naturally brown hair black.

To increase transparency about school rules, all metropolitan senior high schools will also post their regulations on their websites from April.

— *Based on a report on The Asahi Shimbun Asia & Japan Watch on March 15, 2022* —

〈ニュース解説〉　都立高校で、長年合理性に乏しいとされてきた「ブラック校則」の見直しが行われ、5項目の校則が全廃されることになった。「ブラック校則」はもともと、校内暴力が社会問題化した1970年から80年代にかけて生徒を厳しく管理するために規定されたものだが、近年では生徒のプライバシーや人権に関わると問題視されるようになった。都の教育委員会は、今後は生徒たちが主体的に考えてルール作りに参画できる環境を作ることが大事だとしている。

(Notes)　【※☞マークは *Useful Expressions*】

◆　**Tokyo senior highs to retire rules that forced conformity**　「都立高、（ブラック）校則の遵守強制を廃止へ」（ヘッドラインでは通常、未来のことは to 不定詞で表される）

◆　(L. 2)　**relic of the past**　過去の遺物、昔の残物

◆　(L. 3)　**Tokyo metropolitan senior high schools**　都立高校

☞◆　(L. 3)　**do away with**　（制度などを）廃止する、（不要なものを）排除する、なくす

◆　(L. 10)　**undercut hair styles**　「ツーブロック」の髪形（日本語の「ツーブロック」は和製英語）

◆　(L. 10)　**buzz**　（バリカンなどの機械を使って）髪を短く刈りあげる（インターネットや口コミで急速に情報が広がるという意味の日本語の「バズる」は "go viral"）

◆　(L. 11-12)　**go out the window**　完全になくなる（本文の場合は「撤廃される」）

◆　(L. 14)　**the disciplinary measure of forcing problem students to remain at home**　問題を起こした生徒を自宅謹慎させるという懲戒措置（この場合の "of" は同格を表し、of 以下で懲戒措置は校内で別室指導を行うのではなく、自宅で謹慎させるものであることを説明している）

◆　(L. 22)　**Tokyo metropolitan board of education**　東京都教育委員会

◆　(L. 26)　**of the 240 programs available at the 196 metropolitan senior high schools**　都立高校全196校240課程のうち（都立高校には全日制・定時制・通信制の3つの課程がある）

☞◆　(L. 30-31)　**on the grounds that**　〜という理由で

◆　(L. 32)　**needless instructions from teachers about their hair**　髪の毛について教師から不要な指導を受けること（高校卒業後に就職する生徒が多い学校などでは、会社からの評価に関わるため、就職試験や面接などにふさわしい髪の色や髪形を指導する場合が多い）

◆　(L. 34)　**file a lawsuit**　訴訟を起こす、提訴する

1. 本文の内容と一致するものには T (True) を、一致しないものには F (False) を記せ。

(　　　) (1) Five controversial school rules were decided to be abolished since they were unreasonable and unsuitable for current times.

(　　　) (2) All of Tokyo metropolitan senior high schools announced plans to scrap six types of school rules, including the banning of "two-block" undercut hairstyles and submitting a form stipulating hair color and quality.

(　　　) (3) The discussion to review the school rules was held at each school by students without the involvement of teachers.

(　　　) (4) As of April 2022, the metropolitan high schools were to publish their school rules online for the sake of greater transparency.

2. 本文中に掲げた下記の [*Useful Expressions*] を用いて空欄に適語を記し、日本語に合う英文を完成させよ。

(1) ⟨**do away with**⟩

Our society should make every effort to (　　　　　　　　　　　　　).
我々の社会は学校でのいじめをなくすためにあらゆる努力をすべきである。

(2) ⟨**on the grounds that**⟩

She was fired (　　　　　　　　　　　　　) without notice.
彼女は無断欠勤が多いために解雇された。

音声を聞き、下線部を補え。（2回録音されています。1回目はナチュラルスピード、2回目はスロースピードです。）

Natural
♪40
Slow
♪42

Natural
♪41
Slow
♪43

LOS ANGELES—Director Ryusuke Hamaguchi's "Drive My Car" won best international feature film at the 94th US Academy Awards in Los Angeles on Sunday, (1)_____ to bag the prestigious Oscar for the category after having garnered a string of international accolades.

The film depicts a widowed stage actor and director negotiating waves of grief brought on by the sudden death of his wife and (2)_____ _____. He finds solace in the company of a female chauffeur assigned to drive for him (3)_____.

After the ceremony, Hamaguchi said in an interview that (4)_____ _____ that people are living through, as well as the deaths and loss caused by the coronavirus pandemic.

Since winning an award for best screenplay in the famed Cannes film festival in July last year, the three-hour-long drama has received about 90 awards in Japan and abroad.

The triumph of "Drive My Car" reflects (5)_____ _____ by the Oscar, which have been criticized in recent years for lacking diversity.

— Based on a report on a Kyodo News report on March 28, 2022 —

〈ニュース解説〉 第94回アカデミー賞で、濱口竜介監督の「ドライブ・マイ・カー」が国際長編映画賞を受賞した。「ドライブ・マイ・カー」は、世界的に人気の高い村上春樹氏の短編小説を原作に喪失と再生を描いた作品で、作品賞、監督賞、脚色賞の3部門でもノミネートされていた。作品賞にノミネートされるのは日本映画として初めて。同作品は海外の他の映画賞も数多く受賞している。

(Notes)

best international feature film 国際長編映画賞（かつての「外国語映画賞（best foreign language film）」にあたる。米国以外の映画のための賞で、2019年第92回から現在の名称に変更された）　**Academy Awards** アカデミー賞（米国映画芸術科学アカデミーに所属する会員の投票により選定される。国際的な映画賞の最高峰とされるが、近年はダイバーシティの観点からの批判もあった。また、コロナ禍で劇場作品が制限された影響もあって配信による作品も審査対象となり、多くの受賞作品が生まれている）　**Oscar** オスカー像（アカデミー賞の受賞者に与えられる金色の像。"win an Oscar" で「アカデミー賞を取る」の意）　**chauffeur** お抱え運転手（個人に雇われた自家用車の運転手）　**best screenplay** 脚本賞　**Cannes film festival** カンヌ国際映画祭（ベルリン国際映画祭、ヴェネツィア国際映画祭と合わせた世界三大映画祭のひとつ。同映画祭での脚本賞受賞は本作が日本映画として史上初）

■問A 空所 (a) 〜 (j) にそれぞれ入るべき1語を下記の語群から選びその番号を記せ。

体罰	→	(a) punishment
帰国子女	→	(b) children
ひきこもり	→	social (c)
ネットいじめ	→	online (d)
学級崩壊	→	classroom (e)
適応障害	→	(f) disorder
性同一性障害	→	(g) identity disorder
核家族	→	(h) family
育児休暇	→	maternity (i)
共働き世帯	→	(j)-earner household

1. adjustment	2. bullying	3. corporal	4. disintegration
5. dual	6. gender	7. leave	8. nuclear
9. returnee	10. withdrawal		

■問B (a) 〜 (i) にそれぞれ対応する英語表現を下記の語群から選びその番号を記せ。

(a) 不登校	(b) 停学	(c) 過食症
(d) 拒食症	(e) 認知症	(f) 養子縁組
(g) 一神教	(h) 多神教	(i) 無神論

1. adoption	2. anorexia	3. atheism
4. bulimia	5. dementia	6. monotheism
7. polytheism	8. suspension	9. truancy

■問C 空所 (a) 〜 (c) にそれぞれ入るべき1語を下記の語群から選びその番号を記せ。

人間国宝	→	living national (a)
世界文化遺産	→	world cultural (b)
文化勲章	→	(c) of Culture

| 1. heritage | 2. Order | 3. treasure |

From print to the Web — 紙媒体からウェブの重層的構造へ

新聞協会の調査によると、日本における日刊紙発行部数（一般紙とスポーツ紙の双方を含む。朝刊・夕刊セットは1部と計上）は1999年の約5,376万部から2010年には約4,932万部へと減少傾向にある。今後新聞などの紙媒体が消滅してしまうことはないだろうが、ウェブ・ニュース（オンライン・ニュース）には、新聞にはない魅力がある。すなわち、ウェブ・ニュースは様々なメディアの融合体で、新聞のようにニュースを横並びに読むのではなく、ワン・クリックで様々なメディアや情報に重層的にアクセスすることができる。

このトピックを英文で読んでみよう。

Print journalism will not go extinct. But it will become increasingly difficult to compete against the allure of digital media, where editors can combine text, photos, audio, video, animated graphics, interactive chat, and much more. Online media offer readers more variety. Stories, images, and digital extras can be linked together in layers, with related options just a click away. Instead of arranging stories side by side, the way traditional newspapers do, online news sites link related topics in layers that allow readers to roam from story to story.

NEWS MEDIA IN THE WORLD

通信社　News Agencies (3)

✓　ロシア国営のイタル・タス通信（ITAR-TASS）は、ソビエト連邦時代の1925年に誕生したタス通信（TASS）が母体。冷戦期は、政府の公式情報発信機関だったが、ソビエト崩壊後、規模を縮小。中国の新華社通信 "Xinhua News Agency" も国営で中国政府及び共産党の公式見解を報道。政治問題などについて、報道内容や時間的対応状況から、政府の意向や内部事情などを占うことも多い。

NEWS 8

Disk 2

Captain of missing Hokkaido boat forced to sail despite high waves

SHARI, Hokkaido—The president of the operator of a tour boat that went missing off Hokkaido with 26 people aboard last weekend had repeatedly forced captains to depart despite high waves, sources with knowledge of the company's business said Thursday.

The sources said the operator, Shiretoko Yuransen, based in the town of Shari, has been known for frequently going ahead with sightseeing tours despite the chance of bad weather. 5

During a press conference Wednesday, Seiichi Katsurada, the operator's president, admitted that his decision to allow the boat to depart on the condition that its captain would turn back if the seas got rough was "wrong." 10

The sources said Katsurada became angry when captains working for the company canceled tours or were hesitant to sail, citing safety reasons, even before the fatal incident.

The Coast Guard is investigating the incident with the possibility of building a case against the operator on charges of professional negligence resulting in death and endangering traffic. 15

Under Shiretoko Yuransen's rules, it has to cancel tours when the wind speed is expected to exceed 28.8 kilometers per hour and waves are likely to reach a height of 1 meter.

A weather warning for waves over three meters was issued in Shari 20 minutes before Kazu I's departure at 10 a.m. on the day of the accident. 20

Kazu I went missing after leaving port despite the warning to cruise along the peninsula, designated a World Natural Heritage site in 2005 and home to many rare species of animals and plants.

Before contact was lost, the boat, crewed by the 54-year-old captain and a deckhand, told the operator at around 2 p.m. that the vessel was listing 30 degrees, according to the Coast Guard. 25

— Based on a Kyodo News report on April 29,2022 —

〈ニュース解説〉 2022年4月23日、知床半島沖で乗客・乗員26名が乗った観光船「KAZU Ⅰ（カズワン）」が沈没事故を起こした。事故当日は午後から天候の悪化が予想されていたが、運航会社の「知床遊覧船」はツアーを強行し、惨事につながった。事故当時、同社の無線とKAZU Ⅰの衛星電話は故障しており通信手段は携帯電話のみであったが、実際には船長の携帯電話も圏外でつながらない状態だった。航行中の船からの定点連絡も怠っていた事実が明らかになり、同社の安全管理に大きな問題があったことが判明している。

(Notes) 【※☞マークは *Useful Expressions*】

◆ (L. 1) **Shari, Hokkaido** 北海道斜里町（北海道東部、知床半島のオホーツク海に面した町で、雄大な自然を求めて年間約150万人の観光客が訪れている）

☞◆ (L. 2-3) **force captains to depart despite high waves** 高波にもかかわらず船長らに出航を強制する（"force someone to do" は「人に〜するよう強いる、強制する」）

◆ (L. 5) **the operator, Shiretoko Yuransen** 運航会社「知床遊覧船」（"operator" は「運営会社」、または「運営管理者」の意）

☞◆ (L. 6) **go ahead with** （計画・仕事などを）進める、強行する

◆ (L. 8) **Seiichi Katsurada** 桂田精一

◆ (L. 14) **the Coast Guard** 海上保安本部［"coast guard" は一般的には海外における「沿岸警備隊」のことで、有事には軍の指揮下に編入される組織であるが、国土交通省の外局である日本の海上保安庁は「海上の安全及び治安の確保を図る」ことを任務とする警察組織である。長く「Japan Maritime Safety Agency」と称してきたが、近時の領海侵犯事案の多発も踏まえ、国際的に理解しやすい「Japan Coast Guard」に変更した。名称変更後も法律上は軍隊ではなく警察組織であり、武器の使用については警察官職務執行法に従う。海上保安庁は全国を11の管区に分け、それぞれに管区海上保安本部を設置している］

◆ (L. 14-15) **build a case** 立件する

◆ (L. 15) **professional negligence resulting in death** 業務上過失致死罪（業務上必要な注意義務を怠ったり、重大な過失により人を死に至らしめる罪。刑法第211条に定められている）

◆ (L. 16) **endangering traffic** 往来危険罪（船舶の運航に関わる設備を破壊したり、またはそのほかの方法によって艦船の往来の危険を生じさせる行為。刑法第125条に定められている）

◆ (L. 20) **weather warning for waves** 波浪注意報（本文における "warning" は「注意報」の意で用いられているが、厳密には重大な災害が起こるおそれのある場合に警告する「警報」には "warning"、災害が起こるおそれがある場合に予報する「注意報」には "watch" が通例用いられる）

◆ (L. 23) **the peninsula** （知床半島のこと）

◆ (L. 23) **World Natural Heritage site** 世界自然遺産（知床は2005年、流氷が育む豊かな海洋生態系や世界的に希少な動植物の生息地としてユネスコの世界自然遺産に登録された）

◆ (L. 26) **deckhand** 甲板員、（船の）乗組員

◆ (L. 26) **list** （船などが）傾く

1. 本文の内容と一致するものには T (True) を、一致しないものには F (False) を記せ。

(　　) (1) According to the sources, Shiretoko Yuransen frequently sailed even on days when severe weather was forecast.

(　　) (2) The president of the operator said at a press conference that it was the captain's decision to leave port on the fateful day.

(　　) (3) The vessel departed at 10 a.m. and 20 minutes later, a high wave warning was issued in the town of Shari.

(　　) (4) Before contact was lost, Kazu I sent an SOS to the operator saying it was in danger of sinking.

2. 本文中に掲げた下記の［*Useful Expressions*］を用いて空欄に適語を記し、日本語に合う英文を完成させよ。

(1) 〈**force someone to do**〉

The employer (　　　　　　　　　　　　　　) against their wishes.

雇用主は従業員の意に反する過重労働を強いた。　＊過重労働　"excessive work"

(2) 〈**go ahead with**〉

They (　　　　　　　　　　　　　) in spite of the ongoing coronavirus crisis.

彼らはコロナ禍にもかかわらず京都行きを強行した。

音声を聞き、下線部を補え。（２回録音されています。１回目はナチュラルスピード、２回目はスロースピードです。）

Natural
3
Slow
5

The United States was in mourning Wednesday in the aftermath of the country's latest mass killing, (1)_____ in the southwestern state of Texas that left at least 19 children and two adults dead. (2)_____ at a school in the country's history.

The attack unfolded in the small city of Uvalde, where authorities said the 18-year-old gunman first shot his grandmother at her home, (3)_____ _____, carrying out the shootings before law enforcement killed him.

Natural
4
Slow
6

US President Joe Biden, (4)_____ late Tuesday, expressed condolences to the victims' families, while questioning (5)_____ and urging lawmakers to support what he called "common sense gun laws."

"I am sick and tired," he said. "We have to act."

5

10

— *Based on a report on VOANews.com on May 25, 2022* —

〈ニュース解説〉　米国テキサス州の小学校で起きた銃乱射事件で、児童19人と教員2人が犠牲となった。犯行に及んだ地元の男子高校生は、事件直前の18歳の誕生日に殺傷能力の高いアサルトウェポン（殺傷能力の高い突撃銃）を2丁購入したと報じられている。この事件の1か月後、21歳未満の銃購入者に対する身元確認の厳格化などを盛り込んだ銃規制強化法が成立し、約30年ぶりに連邦レベルで銃規制が進むことになった。しかし、ほぼ同時期に、米連邦最高裁判所は厳格な銃規制を設けたニューヨーク州の法律を「武器所持の権利を認めた合衆国憲法修正第2条に違反し、違憲」とする判決を言い渡しており、銃被害を防ぐための取り組みは今後も困難が予想される。（CH6 EX2の関連記事参照）

(Notes)
(be) in mourning 〜の死を悼んで、喪に服して　**in the aftermath of**（災害・戦争などの）直後に　**mass killing** 大量殺人、大虐殺（米国司法省は "mass killing" を「同一の場所・時間帯に同時に3人以上が殺害される犯罪」と定義している）　**in the small city of Uvalde** 小さな町、ユバルディ（"of" は同格を表す。ユバルディはメキシコ国境から90キロほどの場所にある人口約1万6千人の町で、ヒスパニック系の住民が人口の7割を占めている）　**law enforcement** 法執行機関、警察　**express condolences to** 〜に哀悼の意を表す、弔意を表す

■問A　空所 (a) ～ (k) にそれぞれ入るべき1語を下記の語群から選びその番号を記せ。

業務上過失	→	professional (a)
脱税	→	tax (b)
著作権侵害	→	copyright (c)
フィッシング詐欺	→	(d) scam
おとり捜査	→	(e) operation
捜査令状	→	search (f)
物的証拠	→	(g) evidence
状況証拠	→	(h) evidence
精神鑑定	→	(i) test
冤罪	→	(j) charge
自宅軟禁	→	house (k)

1. arrest	2. circumstantial	3. dodge	4. false
5. infringement	6. negligence	7. phishing	8. physical
9. psychiatric	10. sting	11. warrant	

■問B　(a) ～ (q) にそれぞれ対応する英語表現を下記の語群から選びその番号を記せ。

(a) 重罪	(b) 軽犯罪	(c) 違反	(d) 名誉棄損
(e) 拘留	(f) 窃盗	(g) 万引き	(h) スパイ行為
(i) 贈収賄	(j) 監禁	(k) 襲撃	(l) 自白
(m) 大量殺人	(n) 残虐行為	(o) 銃撃	(p) 刺傷
(q) 脱走者			

1. assault	2. atrocity	3. bribery	4. confession
5. confinement	6. custody	7. defamation	8. espionage
9. felony	10. fugitive	11. massacre	12. misdemeanor
13. offense	14. shooting	15. shoplifting	16. stabbing
17. theft			

■問C　(a) ～ (h) をそれぞれ和訳せよ。

(a) abuse	(b) charge	(c) corruption
(d) fraud	(e) interrogation	(f) ransom
(g) robbery	(h) smuggling	

Broadcast news ─ 放送ニュースの特質

放送ニュースは、テレビやラジオの映像や音声を通じて視聴者の感情に訴えることができ、現実を生で伝える力がある。視聴者も面倒な記事を読む煩わしさから解放され、頭を使うことが少なくて済むから大人気。新聞や雑誌といった紙媒体のようなニュースの深みや掘り下げはないが、視聴者へのアピール度や即時性（immediacy）といった面では軍配が上がる。なお、最近では従来のテレビやラジオに加えて、インターネットで聴けるネット・ラジオ、携帯音楽プレイヤーに音声データ・ファイルとして配信される "Podcast"（ポッドキャスト）や携帯電話で視聴できる "One-Seg television"（ワンセグ・テレビ）等、放送ニュースのメディアも実に多様化してきている。

このトピックを英文で読んでみよう。

TV and radio journalism is neither better nor worse than print journalism. It is just different. Each form of media has strengths and weaknesses. Print journalism provides a level of depth, context and sheer information that television and radio newscasts can not supply. Broadcast journalism, through the power of dramatic video and engaging audio, offers an emotional appeal, realism and immediacy that printed stories can not match. Watching or listening to a news broadcast generally requires less intellectual effort than reading a complex news story in a newspaper.

通信社　News Agencies (4)

✓ 日本の共同通信社（Kyodo News Service）と時事通信社（JIJI Press）は第 2 次大戦中の国策通信社・同盟通信社が 1945 年に分割されて出来た。中央、地方の新聞や放送へのニュース記事配信とともに、行政機関や民間会社への情報提供サービスを行っている。近時、アジアを中心に英語による国際的な発信活動にも力を入れている。

NEWS 9

Disk 2 **EDITORIAL: Revised penal code should help in rehabilitation of prison inmates**

The Diet has passed a revision to the penal code to integrate two categories of confinement—*choeki* and *kinko*—into one called *kokin*.

The revision has scrapped the traditional classification into two types of imprisonment, which has been part of the nation's criminal justice system since the Meiji Era (1868-1912).   5

The change is aimed at promoting the rehabilitation of criminals by providing for programs better suited to the needs and characteristics of individual prisoners.

Most of the some 40,000 inmates will be released sooner or later. It is vital to enhance the effectiveness of systems both inside and outside prisons to prepare offenders to successfully reintegrate into society after release so that they will not   10 commit a crime again.

Choeki, which means imprisonment with prison labor, constitutes most of the penalties of confinement for deprivation of liberty meted out in this nation.

Kinko, in comparison, means imprisonment without labor. *Choeki* obliges prisoners to carry out designated work. This inevitably reduces their time for   15 activities useful for rehabilitation, such as reflecting on their life histories or discussions with other inmates.

The revised penal code stipulates that criminals sentenced to the new *kokin* (confinement) penalty can be required to do "work" or receive "guidance." This provides a legal foundation for flexibly combining labor and educational programs   20 for prisoners.

In 2020, 58 percent of all prisoners in Japan were repeat offenders although the ratio has since declined somewhat. In many cases, they return to prison by committing minor crimes as they fail to reintegrate into society. Such cases should be called a kind of "social imprisonment."   25

Our society, for its part, should be more willing to accept released offenders to prevent them from becoming isolated. We should change our mindset and attitude concerning the rehabilitation of inmates while promoting facilities and programs to help them reintegrate into the community.

— Based on a report on The Asahi Shimbun Asia & Japan Watch on June 14, 2022 —

〈ニュース解説〉 懲罰の意味合いが大きかった従来の「懲役刑」と「禁錮刑」が廃止され、受刑者の立ち直りと再犯防止に軸足を置いた「拘禁刑」に一本化されることになった。刑罰の種類が変わるのは現行刑法が 1907 年（明治 40 年）に制定されて以来、初めてのこと。出所後を見据えた支援を行うことで受刑者の社会復帰を後押しし、再犯を防ぐことを目的としている。

(Notes) 【※☞マークは *Useful Expressions*】

◆ **editorial** 社説［一般に、新聞社が社の論説方針に従って政治・経済・社会などの時事問題について意見や主張を述べた論説記事。通常、論説委員が無署名で執筆する。また、米紙等でみられる op-ed（opposite the editorial page）と呼ばれる寄稿欄は、社説の反対側に設けられ、新聞社の支配下にない外部の執筆者が署名付きで意見や見解を述べている］

◆ **revised penal code** 改定刑法

◆ **help in** 〜に役立つ、有効である

◆ **rehabilitation** 社会復帰、更生

◆ **prison inmate** （刑務所に収容されている）受刑者、囚人（単に "inmate" ともいう。後出の "prisoner" も同義）

◆ (L. 1) **integrate** 〜を一体化する、統一する

◆ (L. 2) **confinement** 収監、監禁、閉じ込めること（後出の "imprisonment" も同義）

◆ (L. 4) **criminal justice system** 刑事司法制度

◆ (L. 6) **criminal** 犯罪者（後出の "offender" も同義）

☞◆ (L. 12-13) ***Choeki*, …, constitutes most of the penalties of confinement for deprivation of liberty** 懲役は自由を拘束する収監刑の大半を占める（2020 年に確定した自由拘束刑では、懲役が 99.695％を占めたのに対し、禁錮刑は 0.32％のみであった。"constitute most of" は「〜の大半を占める」）

◆ (L. 13) **mete out** （処罰・裁きなどを）与える、下す

◆ (L. 19) **"guidance"** （ここでは受刑者の更生に必要な指導やプログラムを意味する）

◆ (L. 20) **legal foundation** 法的根拠

◆ (L. 25) **"social imprisonment"** 「社会的入所」（入院による治療の必要がなくなっても帰る家や引き取り手がないために病院で生活を強いられる状態を「社会的入院」と呼ぶことから、社会に適合できず刑務所に戻らざるを得ない状況をこのように呼んでいると思われる）

☞◆ (L. 26) **for its part** 一方〜の側では

◆ (L. 27) **mindset** （習性となっている固定された）考え方、物の見方

1. 本文の内容と一致するものには T (True) を、一致しないものには F (False) を記せ。

(　　) (1) The old law clearly differentiates between inmates who are required to work and those who are not.

(　　) (2) Under the revisions, offenders will be allowed to undergo guidance programs, but will not be allowed to work even if necessary.

(　　) (3) The recidivism rate has been on the rise since 2020.

(　　) (4) In many cases, repeat offenders commit crimes after their release and are sent back to prison due to the difficulty in adjusting to society.

2. 本文中に掲げた下記の［*Useful Expressions*］を用いて空欄に適語を記し、日本語に合う英文を完成させよ。

(1) ⟨**constitute most of**⟩

People over 40 years of age (　　　　　　　　　　　　　　　).

町の人口の大半が 40 歳を超えている。

(2) ⟨**for its part**⟩

(　　　　　　　　　　) as much support as possible to refugees.

一方、日本としてもできる限りの難民支援を行う必要がある。

Natural
9

Slow
11

The Tokyo District Court has ordered Juntendo University (1) _____ (about \$62,500) to 13 women who failed the university's medical school entrance examination after the university adjusted its acceptance criteria to the disadvantage of women.

The 13 women are doctors and former medical students of other universities in their 20s and 30s, living in five prefectures. (2) _____, they had sought a total of approximately 54.7 million yen (about \$425,000) (3) _____. They took the Juntendo University Faculty of Medicine's entrance exams between the 2011 and 2018 academic years.

Natural
10

Slow
12

The third-party committee acknowledged that (4) _____ since the 2013 academic year, in which the admission standard for female and second-time or later candidates (5) _____ who had just graduated from high school.

— *Based on a report on Mainichi.com on May 19, 2022* —

〈ニュース解説〉 順天堂大学医学部の入学試験で「女性に不利な扱いをして不合格としたことは差別だ」と訴えた集団訴訟で、大学側に賠償命令が下された。医学部の入試においては過去にも東京医科大学など複数の大学で女性を不利に扱う判定基準を設けていたことが発覚している。裁判長は「入試目的である医師としての資質や学力の評価と直接の関係がなく、不合理で差別的だ」と非難した。

(Notes)
Tokyo District Court 東京地裁　**Juntendo University** 順天堂大学　**medical school** 医学部（後出の "**Faculty of Medicine**" も同義）　**acceptance criteria** 合格基準、合否判定基準（"criteria" は "criterion" の複数形。後出の admission standard も同義）　**third-party committee** 第三者委員会

■問A　空所 (a) 〜 (i) にそれぞれ入るべき 1 語を下記の語群から選びその番号を記せ。

陪審制度	→	(a) system
裁判員制度	→	(b) system
裁判長	→	(c) judge
国選弁護人	→	(d) lawyer
執行猶予付き判決	→	(e) sentence
終身刑	→	life (f)
死刑	→	death (g)
刑事訴訟	→	(h) action
民事訴訟	→	(i) action

1. civil	2. court-appointed	3. criminal	4. imprisonment
5. jury	6. lay judge	7. penalty	8. presiding
9. suspended			

■問B　(a) 〜 (l) にそれぞれ対応する英語表現を下記の語群から選びその番号を記せ。

(a) 弁護士	(b) 検察官	(c) 原告
(d) 被告	(e) 裁判	(f) 起訴
(g) 証言	(h) 評決	(i) 判決
(j) 有罪判決	(k) 刑罰	(l) 恩赦

1. amnesty	2. conviction	3. defendant	4. judgment
5. lawyer	6. penalty	7. plaintiff	8. prosecution
9. prosecutor	10. testimony	11. trial	12. verdict

■問C　日本の司法制度に関係する (a) 〜 (f) の用語をそれぞれ和訳せよ。

(a) Supreme Court

(b) high court

(c) district court

(d) family court

(e) summary court

(f) Supreme Public Prosecutors Office

Radio news reporting ─ ラジオ・ニュースの難しさ

テレビのような映像がなく、新聞・雑誌のように長々と叙述できないのがラジオのニュース。ラジオの聞き手は何か他のことをしながらラジオ・ニュースを聞いている。そうなると、ニュースも簡潔、そして聞き手の注意を一発で喚起する書き方が要求される。記者には、ニュースを30秒でまとめる技術が求められる。"actuality" または "sound bite"（ニュースで繰り返し放送される録音テープからの抜粋）、"natural sound" または "ambient sound"（周囲の様子を伝えるような音声や環境音）、"lead-in"（ニュース番組の導入部分）等はラジオニュース関連の専門用語。テレビ・ニュースの用語と共通するものも多い。最近はインターネットで聞けるラジオサイトも増え、世界中のラジオ放送を無料で聞くことが出来る。ホームページでは豊富な英文記事の他に、ラジオ・ニュースも聴取できる。BBC World Service（英）、NPR（米）、ABC Radio National（豪）等にアクセスしてオンライン・ラジオ・ニュースを聴いてみよう。

このトピックを英文で読んでみよう。

Radio journalism may be the most challenging form of news reporting. You can not rely on graphics and images as TV reporters do. You can not write long, descriptive sentences and stories as print reporters do. When people are listening to your story on the radio, they are doing it while they dodge traffic, talk on their cellphone, and do their makeup. So radio news writing needs to be as direct and attention-grabbing as possible. Word economy is the key. The best radio reporting is snappy yet eloquent, conversational yet concise, friendly yet authoritative. Most stories at most stations require their reporters to boil everything down to its 30-second essence.

NEWS 10

Disk 2 **Heatwaves becoming normal amid climate change as Europe continues sweltering**

The World Meteorological Organization, WMO, warns heatwaves, raging wildfires and record-breaking temperatures are becoming normal because of climate change.

Meteorologists say the scorching heatwave sweeping Europe is likely to last well into the middle of next week, smashing more temperature records as it continues. ₅ They warn the time between heatwaves is becoming shorter, noting the current event was preceded by a similar one in June. And they say the likelihood of a third heatwave occurring before summer ends is strong.

WMO Secretary-General Petteri Taalas said he has no doubt as to what is behind the phenomenon. ₁₀

"Thanks to climate change, we have started breaking records nationally and also regionally," Taalas said. "In the future, these kinds of heatwaves are going to be normal, and we will see even stronger extremes."

He said people have pumped so much carbon dioxide into the atmosphere that the negative trend will continue for decades. Those who will suffer most, he said, are ₁₅ the elderly and sick. The WMO chief said more frequent, intense heatwaves also will have a major adverse effect on agriculture.

"In the previous heatwaves in Europe, we lost big parts of the harvest, and under the current situation, we are already having this global food crisis," Taalas said. "Because of the war in Ukraine, this heatwave is going to have a further negative ₂₀ impact on agricultural activities."

The World Health Organization's director of environment and health, Maria Neira, said heat compromises the body's ability to regulate its internal temperature. She warned that will lead to a cascade of illnesses, including heat cramps, heat stroke and hyperthermia. ₂₅

Scientists emphasize climate change is happening even faster than drafters of the Paris climate change agreement anticipated. They note warming in many regions already has surpassed 1.5 degrees Celsius above pre-industrial levels.

The WMO's Taalas said the world is heading for 2.5 degrees Celsius warming, which means heatwaves and other extreme weather events will become a normal part ₃₀ of life. He said that should be a wake-up call for human beings.

— Based on a report on VOANews.com on July 19, 2022 —

〈ニュース解説〉 2022年7月、ヨーロッパ諸国は猛烈な熱波に襲われ、英国、フランス、スペイン、ポルトガル等で記録的暑さとなり、山火事が多発、死者も相次いだ。偏西風の蛇行と地球温暖化が原因と言われるが、こうした熱波の襲来は以前より頻繁になっていると専門家は見ている。記録的熱波は北米にも広がり、同月、米テキサス州では過去最高の46.1度を記録した。

(Notes) 【※☞マークは *Useful Expressions*】

☞◆ **Heatwaves becoming normal amid climate change as Europe continues sweltering** 「うだるような暑さが続く欧州諸国、気候変動で熱波が常態化」（ヘッドラインではしばしば be 動詞が省略されるが、ここでも Heatwaves are becoming ～の "are" が省略されている）（p13 The headline―「見出し」の特徴を参照のこと）

◆ (L. 1) **World Meteorological Organization** 世界気象機関（気象、気候、水に関する権威のある科学情報を提供する国連の専門機関。地球の大気の状態と動き、大陸と海洋の相互作用、気象とそれが作り出す気候、その結果による水資源の分布等を観測、監視するための国際協力を調整している。略称は WMO、本部はスイスのジュネーブ）

◆ (L. 2) **record-breaking temperatures** （2022年7月には英国・フランスで 40℃以上、ポルトガルで 47℃以上、スペインでも 45℃という記録的な暑さとなった）

☞◆ (L. 4) **sweeping** 広範の、全面的な、（勝利などが）圧倒的な［英語ニュースで頻出するが、"sweep" の原義は（ほうきで）掃く］

◆ (L. 9) **WMO Secretary-General Petteri Taalas** ペッテリ・ターラス WMO 事務局長

◆ (L. 13) **even stronger extremes** さらに猛烈な熱波などのより激しい異常気象

◆ (L. 15) **the negative trend** （最高気温の記録更新が続くような現在の傾向を意味する）

◆ (L. 16) **the WMO chief** （ターラス WMO 事務局長を指す）

◆ (L. 22-23) **World Health Organization's director of environment and health, Maria Neira** マリア・ネイラ世界保健機関公衆衛生環境局長（世界保健機関は「全ての人々が可能な限りの最高の健康水準に到達すること」を目的として設立された国連の専門機関。略称は WHO、本部はスイスのジュネーブ）

◆ (L. 24) **heat cramp** 熱性痙攣

◆ (L. 24) **heat stroke** 熱中症、熱射病

◆ (L. 25) **hyperthermia** 高熱、高体温

☞◆ (L. 27) **the Paris climate change agreement** ［2015年に開催された第21回国連気候変動枠組み条約締約国会議（COP21）で採択されたパリ協定（Paris Agreement）のこと。世界共通の長期目標として気温の上昇を産業革命以前のレベルから 2℃できれば 1.5℃に留めるべく温暖化ガスの削減に努める等が定められた］

☞◆ (L. 28) **1.5 degrees Celsius** 摂氏 1.5 度、1.5℃［"Celsius" は摂氏のシステムを作った学者名に由来。"C" は "centigrade" と表現されることもある。欧米で日常的に使われることの多い華氏（"Fahrenheit"、略語 F）もこのシステムを作った学者名に因む］

◆ (L. 28) **pre-industrial levels** 産業革命以前のレベル

◆ (L. 31) **wake-up call** 警鐘、注意喚起（原義はホテルなどのモーニングコール）

1. 本文の内容と一致するものには T (True) を、一致しないものには F (False) を記せ。

(   ) (1) The heatwave hit only a small part of Europe in July 2022.

(   ) (2) Experts predict that as many as three intense heatwaves will happen in Europe in summer of 2022.

(   ) (3) The WMO chief believes that heatwaves in Europe are the only reason for the current global food crisis.

(   ) (4) Heat damages the temperature control system in the human body.

(   ) (5) The WMO chief warns that there is a possibility that the world temperature will exceed 2.5℃ above the pre-industrial levels.

2. 本文中に掲げた ［*Useful expression*］〈**sweeping**〉を用いて、下記の語群を並び替えて空欄に適語を記し、日本語に合う英文を完成させよ。

(1) その会社は収益性を向上させるために全面的な改革を実施した。

The company (   ) (   ) (   )
(   ) (   ) (   ) (   ).

implemented,	improve,	its,	profitability,
reforms,	sweeping,	to	

(2) その与党は総選挙で圧倒的な勝利を収めた。

The ruling party (   ) (   ) (   )
(   ) (   ) (   ) (   )
(   ).

a,	in,	election,	general,	scored,
sweeping,	the,	victory		

Natural 15 **Slow** 17

TOKYO—Japan's top automakers are gearing up to roll out electric versions of the lightweight *kei* minicars that are so popular with drivers in the country, [1] _____ in the world's No. 3 economy.

Nissan Motor and Mitsubishi Motors are leading the race to electrify the tiny, nippy cars that are unique to the roads of Japan and [2] _____ . They plan to launch an electric *kei* car developed by their NMKV joint venture early [3] _____ .

Natural 16 **Slow** 18

The joint venture's new model will travel 170 km on a single charge and cost at least 2 million yen ($17,500) after government subsidies. That's a much smaller range than the up to 610 km offered by Nissan's first all-electric crossover sport utility vehicle, the Ariya, but the [4] _____ of 5.39 million yen.

According to a survey by the Japan Automobile Manufacturers Association, 75% of *kei* car owners drive "almost every day" [5] _____ . They have also become indispensable in helping some people get to places like hospitals, banks and other public facilities.

— *Based on a report on Nikkei Asia.com on January 31, 2022* —

5

10

15

〈ニュース解説〉　日本の主要自動車メーカーは 2050 年までにカーボンニュートラル社会を実現することを目指し、軽自動車サイズの電気自動車の開発を進めてきたが、日産と三菱自動車が 2022 年夏その先陣を切って軽 EV を発売する予定。日常使いで街乗りという「軽」の特性を考え、バッテリーの航続距離を抑えてコストダウンを図り、今後の軽 EV の普及を目指している。2021 年の日本の新車販売に占める軽自動車の割合は 37.1 パーセントを占めるため、脱炭素に向けての大きなインパクトが見込まれる。

(Notes)

lightweight *kei* minicars 軽自動車（英語以外の外国語はしばしばイタリックで表記される。ここの "kei" も日本語の「軽」を示している）　**Nissan Motor and Mitsubishi Motors**（日産自動車株式会社と三菱自動車工業株式会社。二社は資本提携関係にある。正式名称はそれぞれ "Nissan Motor Corporation" と "Mitsubishi Motors Corporation"）　**tiny, nippy cars** 小型で小回りのきく自動車　**unique to the roads of Japan**（日本には軽自動車しか相互走行できない細い道が多数存在するという特殊事情があるとされることを意味する）　**NMKV** エヌエムケーブイ（日産と三菱自動車が共同出資して設立した軽自動車に特化したジョイント・ベンチャー）　**government subsidies**（政府はクリーン・エネルギー自動車を普及促進するため、通常の EV 購入者には最大 80 万円、軽 EV 購入者にも最大 50 万円の補助金を供与している）　**Nissan's first all-electric crossover sport utility vehicle, the Ariya**［日産が初めて発売したクロスオーバー EV「アリヤ」。クロスオーバーとは街乗りでの快適性を重視した都市型の SUV（スポーツ用多目的車）］　**Japan Automobile Manufacturers Association** 日本自動車工業会（自動車、バイク等を日本国内で製造する 14 社から成る業界団体）

■問A 空所 (a) ～ (g) にそれぞれ入るべき 1 語を下記の語群から選びその番号を記せ。

光化学スモッグ　　 → 　(a) smog

生物多様性　　　　 → 　biological (b)

排ガス規制　　　　 → 　(c) control

放射性廃棄物　　　 → 　(d) waste

絶滅危惧種　　　　 → 　(e) species

永久凍土の溶解　　 → 　(f) thawing

産業革命前の気温　 → 　(g) temperature

> 1. diversity,　　　 2. emission,　　 3. endangered,　 4. permafrost,
> 5. photochemical,　 6. pre-industrial,　 7. radioactive

■問B　(a) ～ (r) をそれぞれ和訳せよ。

(a)　ecosystem

(b)　ozone layer depletion

(c)　environmentalist

(d)　environmentally friendly

(e)　pollutant

(f)　deforestation

(g)　desertification

(h)　greenhouse gas

(i)　extreme weather

(j)　cold wave

(k)　Japan Meteorological Agency

(l)　flood warning

(m)　rescuers

(n)　drought

(o)　evacuation center

(p)　volcanic eruption

(q)　aftershock

(r)　tidal wave

Media convergence — メディアの融合化への流れ

> 昨今のジャーナリズムは、マルチメディアを駆使して情報を伝達する。1つのことを伝えるにも、写真、オーディオ、ビデオ（動画）、テキスト（文字データ）というようにあらゆる媒体を使って、より理想に近い情報を作り出し伝達することが出来るのがメディア融合の強みである。

このトピックを英文で読んでみよう。

Suppose you decided to profile Ludwig van Gogh, a brilliant painter and composer. Which medium, or media, would produce the best story? To display his paintings, you would use photographs. To present his music, you would use audio recordings. To show him at work—conducting an orchestra or painting—you would use video footage. To explain the meaning and impact of his art, you would use text. In short, to create the ideal profile, you would need multimedia. Cross-platform journalism, media convergence—whatever you call it, it is an idea whose time has finally come.

NEWS MEDIA IN THE WORLD

新聞社 Newspapers (1)

✔ 英国では、庶民を読者とする大衆紙には昔からタブロイド判（tabloid）が多いが、これまで大判（broadsheet）で出されていた高級紙 *Times* や *Guardian* も判型をタブロイド判に変えつつある。2015 年以降日本経済新聞傘下にある高級経済紙 *Financial Times*（略称 FT）は大判でピンク色の用紙が特徴。近年経費削減等の理由から紙面の縮小が流行で、*Guardian* やフランスの *Le Monde* など、大判とタブロイド判の中間の大きさのベルリーナ判（Berliner format）を採用する新聞もあった。*Guardian* は、その後 2018 年に判型をベルリーナ判からタブロイド判に変更し、*Times* と並び英国高級紙のタブロイド判化として話題となった。

NEWS 11

UN warns of 'looming hunger catastrophe' due to Russian blockade

A looming hunger catastrophe is set to explode over the next two years, creating the risk of unprecedented global political pressure, the executive director of the UN World Food Programme has warned.

Calling for short- and long-term reforms—including an urgent lifting of the blockade on 25m tonnes of Ukrainian grain trapped by a Russian blockade—David 5 Beasley said the current food affordability crisis is likely to turn into an even more dangerous food availability crisis next year unless solutions are found.

The number of people classed as "acutely food insecure" by the UN before the Covid crisis was 130 million, but after Covid this number rose to 276 million.

Writing a preface to a new pamphlet from the Blair Institute on the looming 10 hunger crisis, Beasley says: "This number has increased to 345 million due to the Ukraine crisis. And a staggering 50 million people in 45 countries are now just one step from famine. The international community must act to stop this looming hunger catastrophe in its tracks or these numbers will explode. Global food markets have been plunged into turmoil, with soaring prices, export bans and shortages of basic 15 foodstuffs spreading far from Ukraine's borders. Nations across Africa, the Middle East, Asia and even Latin America are feeling the heat from this conflict."

Beasley says that threats to global food security have been exacerbated by the upheaval in worldwide fuel and fertiliser markets.

"Without urgent action, food production and crop yields will be slashed. This 20 raises the frightening possibility that on top of today's food-pricing crisis, the world will also face a genuine crisis of food availability over the next 12 to 24 months— and with it, the spectre of multiple famines."

— Based on a report on The Guardian.com on July 8, 2022 —

〈ニュース解説〉 異常気象、紛争、コロナ禍等により世界的に食料不安が高まっている。2022年にはロシアが「世界の食料庫」と呼ばれるウクライナに侵攻した影響を受け、穀物をはじめとする食料価格が過去10年来の最高値をつけるまでに高騰、特に貧困層に大打撃が及んだ。ロシアとウクライナ合計で小麦・大麦の世界生産量の3割を占めており、今後もウクライナの農業インフラや港湾への打撃、西側諸国の対ロ経済制裁の影響等により世界の食料供給事情が一層深刻化することが懸念される。

(Notes) 【※☞マークは *Useful Expressions*】

☞◆ **looming** 不気味に迫ってきている、迫りくる［原義は「蜃気楼で遠くの物が浮かび上がって見える」ことを示す。英語ニュース頻出語で Cambridge Dictionary は "(Of something unwanted or unpleasant) about to happen and causing worry" と定義している］

◆ **blockade** 封鎖（ウクライナに侵攻したロシア軍による黒海封鎖を指す）

◆ **catastrophe** 破滅的状況、大惨事

☞◆ (L. 1-2) **…, creating the risk of ～** （英語ニュースではこのように主部の後ろに来る分詞構文が頻出し、「…、そして～する」と言った意味となる）

◆ (L. 2-3) **executive director of the UN World Food Programme** 国連世界食糧計画（WFP）事務局長（後出の David Beasley 氏を指す。WFP は飢餓のない世界を目指して活動する国連の食料支援機関。紛争や自然災害などの緊急時に食料支援を行うとともに、途上国の地域社会と協力して栄養状態の改善と強い社会づくりに取り組んでいる。本部はイタリア・ローマ。"programme" は英国式綴り。米国式綴りは "program"）

◆ (L. 4-5) **the blockade on 25 million tonnes of Ukrainian** （ウクライナの主要積出港であるオデーサ等へのアクセスがロシア側の攻撃に阻まれ、2022年7月現在、2500万トンの穀物が輸出できない状態にあることを指す。"ton" の複数形 "tonnes" は英国式綴り。米国式綴りは "tons"）

◆ (L. 5-6) **David Beasley** デビッド・ビーズリー

◆ (L. 6) **food affordability crisis** （手が届くような価格で食料を確保することができなくなるような危機的状況）

◆ (L. 7) **food availability** （適切な品質の食料が十分な量だけ供給できなくなる危機的状態。食料危機が "food affordability crisis" よりさらに悪化した状態を指す）

◆ (L. 8) **acutely food insecure** 急性食料不安（WFP によると、急性食料不安とは、「十分な食料を摂取できないことで、その人の生命や生活が差し迫った危険にさらされること」を意味する）

◆ (L. 10) **Blair Institute** トニー・ブレア・グローバル・チェンジ研究所（Tony Blair Global Change Institute トニー・ブレア元英国首相が設立した非営利研究所）

◆ (L. 12) **a staggering 50 million people** 驚愕するような5000万人に及ぶ人々（複数名詞に "a" が付されているのは、この人数の人々を一まとまりの集団と見なしているため。"a staggering number of ～" とも表現できる）

☞◆ (L. 15) **…, with soaring prices, exports bans ～** （カンマの後は付帯状況を示すために使われる "with" の用例で、英語ニュースに頻出。追加情報を示すことができる）

◆ (L. 18) **food security** 食糧安全保障［国連食糧農業機関（FAO）は「全ての人が、いかなる時にも、活動的で健康的な生活に必要な食生活上のニーズと嗜好を満たすために、十分で安全かつ栄養ある食料を、物理的、社会的及び経済的にも入手可能であるときに達成される状況」と定義］

◆ (L. 23) **spectre of multiple famines** （世界の様々な場所で飢饉が生じる不安。"spectre" は英国式綴り。米国式綴りは "specter"。原義は「幽霊、亡霊」。だが、ここでは「不安」や「不愉快な見通し」）

1. 本文の内容と一致するものには T (True) を、一致しないものには F (False) を記せ。

(   ) (1) A food affordability crisis is more serious than a food availability crisis.

(   ) (2) The WFP executive director warned that the global food insecurity would be more serious unless Russian lifts the blockade on Ukrainian grain.

(   ) (3) The number of people classified as "acutely food insecure" has more than doubled than that before the Covid-19 pandemic.

(   ) (4) People in Latin American countries have not been affected by the current food affordability crisis.

(   ) (5) The current global fuel and fertilizer market disorder has also contributed to worsening global food security.

2. 本文中に掲げた［*Useful Expression*］を参照し、下記の語群を並び替えて空欄に適語を記し、日本語文に合う英文を完成させよ。

(1) 〈**looming** を用いて〉

米国の投資家は差し迫る景気後退を懸念している。

Investors in the US (   ) (   ) (   ) (   ) (   ) (   ).

> a,　about,　are,　looming,　recession,　worried

(2) 〈…, with 〜（付帯状況を示す表現）も用いて〉

昨日の関東地方はこの季節らしい暑さで、気温は 30 度まで上がった。

It was (   ) (   ) (   ) (   ) (   ) (   ) (   ) (   ) (   ) (   ) to 30 degrees Celsius.

> in,　hot,　Kanto,　region,　rising,　seasonably,
> temperatures,　the,　with,　yesterday

音声を聞き、下線部を補え。（２回録音されています。１回目はナチュラルスピード、２回目はスロースピードです。）

Natural
21
Slow
23

Prime Minister Fumio Kishida instructed his Cabinet on Jan. 18 to draw up a new clean energy strategy for the country (1)_____ a carbon-neutral society.

Kishida intends to promote the development of nuclear technology, not just renewable energy, through the strategy, which he hopes to make a (2)_____ _____, which he is calling "new capitalism." 5

"Climate change is an issue where negative aspects of capitalism, including a lack of sustainability, are concentrated," Kishida said in a meeting with experts held in the prime minister's office the same day and told them he would like to share with them the (3)_____. 10

Natural
22
Slow
24

Kishida added that he intends to at least double investment in this area.Japan is aiming to reach net-zero carbon emissions by 2050, but that target will heap an extra burden on (4)_____—for example, by requiring them to overhaul their operations.

Other issues the government considers important include (5)_____ 15 _____ of huge amounts of renewable energy, making use of hydrogen and ammonia as zero-emission energy sources, and changing people's lifestyles and consumption habits.

— *Based on a report on The Asahi Shimbun Asia & Japan Watch on January 19, 2022* —

〈ニュース解説〉　2022 年 1 月、岸田政権は「クリーンエネルギー戦略」を首相主導の主要課題と新たに位置づけ、同政権が掲げる「新しい資本主義」の推進力として行く方針を固めた。具体的には、再生可能エネルギー普及のための送電網増強、電気自動車用蓄電池の拡充、省エネに適したライフスタイルへの転換、温暖化ガスの排出に価格を付し削減を促進するカーボンプライシング等の実現が目指されることになる。

(Notes)
carbon neutral カーボン（後出の "net-zero emission" も同義）　**"new capitalism"** 新しい資本主義（2021 年秋に発足した岸田政権の看板政策。競争原理を重視する新自由主義の下で公平な分配が行われずに格差拡大を招いたとして「成長と分配の好循環」を通じた分厚い中間層の復活を目指すとしている）　**a meeting with experts**（「クリーンエネルギー戦略に関する有識者懇談会」の初会合のこと）　**prime minister's office** 首相官邸

■問A (a) ～ (n) をそれぞれ和訳せよ。

(a) solar cell

(b) renewable energy

(c) geothermal power production

(d) wave-energy power station

(e) hydroelectric power plant

(f) nuclear power generation

(g) thermal power generation

(h) biofuel

(i) fossil fuel

(j) energy conservation

(k) power grid

(l) power shortage

(m) blackout

(n) liguified natural gas

■問B 空所 (a) ～ (g) にそれぞれ入るべき1語を下記の語群から選び記せ。

(a) 食料自給率   food self-(   ) ratio

(b) 食料安全保障   food (   )

(c) 食料不足   food (   )

(d) 廃棄食料   food (   )

(e) 余剰食料   food (   )

(f) 無添加食品   non-(   ) food

(g) 有機食品   (   ) food

1. additive,   2. organic,   3. security,   4. shortage,
5. sufficiency,   6. surplus,   7. waste

Chapter 1-10 ではニュースの定義から始めて、ニュースの種類、ニュースの構成要素と組み立て方といったポイントを概観すると共に、紙媒体のニュース、オンラインニュース、映像や音声で伝えるニュースの特質と、これらのニュースの融合化の流れを紹介した。Chapter 11-15 ではジャーナリストがひとつひとつの表現や文章を書く上で留意すべき 5 つの重要点を検討する。

Passive verbs — 受身の動詞

即時性や解り易さを旨とする英文ジャーナリズムの世界では、より直接的で、迫力のある文章を作るため、能動態を用い、動詞の受身用法（be ＋過去分詞）は避けるべき、というのが常識。
受身用法は、

➢ 主張内容があいまいになり、文章にインパクトがなくなる
➢ 主語や主体がわかりにくく、誰の意見か不明で無責任な内容になりやすい
➢ There is ～や There are ～を使う表現は読者に迂遠で慇懃な感じを与える
➢ 能動態より be 動詞と動作主を示す by が増えることで文章が長くなる

などのデメリットがある。
パンチのあるニュース記事を書くためには、力強く、直接的でイメージのわく動詞を選ぶ事も大切だ。

このトピックを英文で読んでみよう。

There is a problem many reporters struggle with. The sentences that are written by them are passive. Their phrasing is made awkward because of this, and—wait! *Stop!*

Let's rewrite that paragraph to make it less *passive*:

Many reporters struggle because they write passive sentences. This makes their phrasing awkward.

See the difference? We have strengthened our syntax by starting sentences with their subjects. We have eliminated that clunky phrase *there is*. And we have replaced the verb *to be* (words such as *is* and *are*), with stronger verbs.

You do not have to be a grammar geek to see our point here. Make your sentences *emphatic*. Avoid weak, flabby verbs.

NEWS MEDIA IN THE WORLD

新聞社 Newspapers (2)

✔ 米国の新聞は発行部数の少ない地域紙が主流。リベラルな高級紙といわれる *New York Times* や *Washington Post*、*Los Angeles Times* も地方紙だ。米国では、地方紙で研鑽を積んだ記者が高級紙や全国放送の記者に採用されるのが一般的。1980 年代に全米を対象に創刊された *USA Today* も各地域のニュースをフォロー。経済紙の *Wall Street Journal*（略称 WSJ）は、経済通信社の Dow Jones の所有。保守的論調で知られる。

NEWS 12

Disk 2

UN: Global population to reach 8 billion this year, India to become most populated country

The world is continuing to grow. The latest report from the United Nations projects the global population will reach 8 billion people later this year and continue to rise for the next eight decades.

The World Population Prospects 2022 report, released on Monday by the UN's Department of Economic and Social Affairs Population Division, outlined what 5 countries around the world should expect in the coming years.

The global population is expected to reach 8 billion by Nov. 15, the UN predicts, but it won't stop there. The population could be around 8.5 billion by 2030, 9.7 billion in 2050, and 10.4 billion in 2100, meaning Earth could have a 31% increase in human population by the end of the century. 10

The estimated population growth comes as the world's average fertility rate continues to decline. In 2020, the global population growth rate fell below 1% for the first time since 1950. Currently, it's at 2.3 births per woman, down from the average five births per woman in 1950. By 2050, it's expected to slightly fall to 2.1 births per woman. 15

Still, factors such as the rise of life expectancy are reasons why the global population continues to rise.

"Globally, life expectancy reached 72.8 years in 2019, an increase of almost 9 years since 1990. Further reductions in mortality are projected to result in an average longevity of around 77.2 years globally in 2050," the report reads. 20

People ages 65 and older are expected to account for 16% of the human population by 2050, up from 10% in 2022. Men currently make up 50.3% of the population, but by 2050, there are expected to be just as many women as men.

China has long been the most populous country, but that isn't expected to last long, with India projected to be the world's most populous country in 2023. Each 25 country currently has a population over 1.4 billion people, accounting for over 35% of the global population, but China's population is expected to start declining as early as next year. By 2050, India is projected to have 1.6 billion people, while China is projected to have 1.3 billion people.

— Based on usatoday.com on July 11, 2022 —

〈ニュース解説〉 世界人口はその増加率は鈍化してきているものの、2022 年 11 月には 80 億人となる見通し。その後、2030 年には 85 億人、2050 年には 97 億人へと増加が続くが、2080 年代に 104 億人でピークに達すると予想されている。2023 年にはインドの人口が中国を抜いて最多になる見込み。インドでは出生率が高いだけでなく、乳幼児死亡率（5 歳未満の死亡率）が下がってきていることなどがその要因とされる。一方、現在人口が最多の中国では 1970 年代に導入された一人っ子政策などの影響で出生数は低下してきている。なお、合計特殊出生率は 2010 年代前半をピークに先進国を中心に低下傾向が続く。

(Notes)　【※☞マークは *Useful Expressions*】

☞◆ **UN: Global population to reach 8 billion this year, India to become most populated country**　国連推計：世界人口 2022 年に 80 億人、インド人口最多国に。[この見出しには① コロンで情報源を示す、② to 不定詞で未来形を示す、③ and の代わりにカンマを使用する、④ 略語が多用される（UN は United Nations の略）等の見出し特有の表現方法が見られる]（「見出し」の特徴：p13 を参照のこと）

◆ (L. 1)　**the latest report from the United Nations**　［後出の "The World Population Prospects 2022 report"（国連世界人口推計 2022 年版）を指す］

◆ (L. 4-5)　**UN's Department of Economic and Social Affairs Population Division**　国連経済社会局（UNDESA）人口部

◆ (L.11)　**comes as**　（ここでは "is happening at the same time that" の意味）

◆ (L. 11)　**fertility rate**　［"total fertility rate"（合計特殊出生率）のこと。15 歳〜49 歳の女性 1 人が生涯に産む子供の数の平均値を意味する］

☞◆ (L. 16)　**life expectancy**　平均寿命（0 歳における平均余命のこと。後出の "average longevity" も同義）

☞◆ (L. 19)　**mortality (rate)**　死亡率（"death rate" と同義）

◆ (L. 21)　**account for 〜**　〜を占める（後出の "make up" と同義）→ Useful Expression 4（英語ニュース頻出語 "account for 〜"）

◆ (L. 25)　**—, with India projected to be the world's most populous country in 2023**　（付帯状況を示す "with" の用法については Chapter 11 News 11 の Useful Expression 3 を参照のこと）

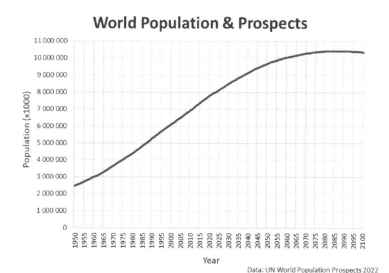

World Population & Prospects

Data: UN World Population Prospects 2022

1. 本文の内容と一致するものには T (True) を、一致しないものには F (False) を記せ。

(　　　) (1) The global population is expected to be bigger than 8 billion people in 2023.

(　　　) (2) The UN predicts that the world population will surpass 10 billion in 2100.

(　　　) (3) The rate of increase in global population has slowed down recently as the world's average total fertility rate has kept falling.

(　　　) (4) The share of people aged 65 and older is expected to increase by 6 percentage points during the period from 2022 and 2050.

(　　　) (5) At present, China and India make up less than one-third of the global population.

2. 本文中に掲げた [*Useful expression*] 〈**mortality rate**〉（死亡率）とは「ある集団に属する人のうち、一定期間中に死亡した人の割合」を意味するが、下記は米国疾病予防センター（CDC）による「乳児死亡率」に関する説明の一部である。空所 (1) 〜 (6) に入るべき適語を語群から選び答えよ。

Infant mortality is the death of an infant (¹·　　　　　) his or her (²·　　　　　) birthday. The infant mortality rate is the number of infant deaths for (³·　　　　　) 1,000 live (⁴·　　　　　). In addition to giving us key (⁵·　　　　　) about maternal and infant health, the infant mortality rate is an important marker of the overall health of a (⁶·　　　　　). In 2020, the infant mortality rate in the United States was 5.4 deaths per 1,000 live births.

after,	births,	before,	deaths,	every,
first,	information,	second,	some,	society

Natural
(27)
Slow
(29)

Natural
(28)
Slow
(30)

　　　The number of births in 2021 in Japan fell by 3.5% from the previous year to 811,604, hitting the lowest level on record, according to data released by the Ministry of Health, Labour and Welfare on Friday.

　　　That figure has been falling since 2016, when it first dropped below 1 million, and [(1)] _____ below 800,000.　　　　5

　　　Japan's total fertility rate, which indicates [(2)] _____ _____ on average, also fell 0.03 point to 1.30 in 2021 from the previous year.

　　　This marks the sixth straight year the number has declined. The figure fell further from 2020, when the impact of the Covid-19 pandemic was most evident,　　10 reaching its fourth-lowest point [(3)] _____ _____.

　　　After falling below 2.00 in 1975, the fertility rate has consistently trended downward, reaching a nadir of 1.26 in 2005. From that point it has risen gradually as [(4)] _____ reached childbearing age,　　15 increasing to 1.45 in 2015.

　　　However, more recently, the number of marriages has begun declining as people [(5)] _____. This trend, combined with a drop in marriages because of the pandemic, means the birth rate has not trended upward.　　　　20

　　　　　　　　　　　　—*Based on a report on Nikkei Asia.com on June 3, 2022*—

〈ニュース解説〉　2021 年の日本の出生数は 81 万 1604 人と 6 年連続で過去最少を記録した。女性一人が一生のうちに産む子供の数の平均を示す合計特殊出生率も 1.30 と前年からさらに 0.03 ポイント減少し、6 年連続での低下となった。一方、出生数から死亡者数を差し引いた人口の自然減は 62 万 8205 人と過去最大を記録した。

(Notes)
total fertility rate 合計特殊出生率（この数値が 2 を下回ると人口は減少へと向かうことになる）　**nadir** 最低値、最悪 [原義は「天空」。「天頂」（zenith）の反対語]

■問A　空所 (a) ～ (i) にそれぞれ入るべき1語を下記の語群から選びその番号を記せ。

合計特殊出生率	→	total (a) rate
死亡率	→	(b) rate
人口密度が高い地域	→	(c) populated area
人口密度が低い地域	→	(d) populated area
人口過密地域	→	(e) area
過疎化地域	→	(f) area
人口動向	→	(g) trend
少子高齢化	→	(h) birthrate and (i) population

1. aging　2. declining　3. demographic　4. densely　5. depopulated
6. fertility　7. mortality　8. overpopulated　9. sparsely

■問B　(a) ～ (m) をそれぞれ和訳せよ。

(a) equal employment opportunity

(b) emerging countries

(c) least developed countries

(d) income gap

(e) minimum wage

(f) health insurance

(g) nursing home

(h) gerontology

(i) working age population

(j) workforce（あるいは labor force）

(k) dependent

(l) spouse

(m) paternal leave

Redundancy — 冗長な文章を避ける

不必要な語や表現を使用すると文章は冗長になる。例えば、形容詞と名詞の組み合わせでは、名詞にその形容詞の意味がもとから含まれている場合にその表現は冗長となる。副詞と動詞の組み合わせにおいても、動詞がその副詞の意味を持つ場合に同様の問題が発生する。ニュースルームでは、記者が作成したニュース原稿は編集デスクに送られ文体や内容のチェックを受けた後、報道される。

このトピックを英文で読んでみよう。

Sometimes it is not so obvious that you are using unnecessary words and phrases. Why say that someone is *currently* president of the club? Or that the game is *scheduled for* Friday night? Or that the victims were burned *in the flames*?

Those italicized words add bulk, but no extra meaning. Just as bad are phrases such as these, which are simply doublespeak:

grateful thanks	true fact	personal opinion
all-time record	end result	serious danger
totally destroyed	very unique	first time ever

Be on the lookout for unnecessary modifiers that *sound* logical but add nothing. Eliminate waste. Edit yourself ruthlessly. As Mark Twain once advised: "When in doubt, strike it out."

NEWS MEDIA IN THE WORLD

新聞社 Newspapers (3)

✔ ロシアのプラウダ（*Pravda*）、中国の人民日報（*People's Daily*）はいずれも両国共産党の機関紙として出発。ソビエト崩壊や中国の近代化により情報発信の多様化が進んだが、報道活動に一定の制限がある中国では政府の意向を窺うメディアとして依然重要。アジアでは、シンガポールの英字紙 *Straits Times* や華字紙の『聯合早報』、タイの英字紙 *Nation*、日本の英字紙 *Japan Times* 等がある。FT や WSJ のアジア版、*New York Times* の世界版である *International New York Times*（かつての *International Herald Tribune*）等が各地で印刷発行されている。

NEWS 13

Disk 2
(31)

Amino acids found in asteroid samples collected by Japan's Hayabusa2 probe

More than 20 types of amino acids have been detected in samples Japan's Hayabusa2 space probe brought to Earth from an asteroid in late 2020, a government official said Monday, showing for the first time the organic compounds exist on asteroids in space. With amino acids essential for all living things to make proteins, the discovery could hold clues to understanding the origins of life, the education 5 ministry said.

In December 2020, a capsule that had been carried on a six-year mission by Hayabusa2 delivered more than 5.4 grams of surface and subsurface materials to Earth from the Ryugu asteroid, located over 300 million kilometers away. The probe of Ryugu was aimed at unraveling the mysteries of the origin of the solar system 10 and life. Previous analysis of the samples had suggested the presence of water and organic matter.

The full-fledged investigation of the sample was launched in 2021 by the Japan Aerospace Exploration Agency and research institutions nationwide including the University of Tokyo and Hiroshima University. Although it is not known how amino 15 acids arrived on ancient Earth, one theory says they were brought by meteorites, with amino acids being detected in a meteorite found on Earth.

But there is also a possibility that they were attached on the ground. Meteors that reach Earth burn up when they hit the atmosphere, and quickly become contaminated with terrestrial microorganisms. Hayabusa2 was groundbreaking in that it collected 20 subsurface materials not weathered by sunlight or cosmic rays, and delivered them to Earth unexposed to outside air.

Kensei Kobayashi, professor emeritus of astrobiology at Yokohama National University, said the unprecedented discovery of multiple types of amino acids on an extraterrestrial body could even hint at the existence of life outside of Earth. 25 "Proving amino acids exist in the subsurface of asteroids increases the likelihood that the compounds arrived on Earth from space," he said. It also means amino acids can likely be found on other planets and natural satellites, hinting that "life could have been born in more places in the universe than previously thought," Kobayashi added.

Hayabusa2 left Earth in 2014 and reached its stationary position above Ryugu in 30 June 2018 after traveling 3.2 billion km on an elliptical orbit around the Sun for more than three years. The probe touched down on the asteroid twice the following year, collecting the first-ever subsurface samples from an asteroid.

— Based on a report on Kyodo News report on June 6, 2022 —

〈ニュース解説〉　2014年12月、宇宙航空研究開発機構（JAXA）の小惑星探査機「はやぶさ2」が種子島宇宙航空センターから小惑星「リュウグウ」に向けて打ち上げられた。地球から3億キロ以上離れた直径900メートルのリュウグウに着陸したのが2019年2月で、地表の岩石や砂のサンプルが収集された。同年4月には上空からリュウグウに重さ2キロの金属弾が打ち込まれ、直径数メートルのクレーターが作られた。太陽光や宇宙（放射）線で「宇宙風化」していない物質を地表下から周辺に噴出させる狙いで、7月に再着陸して、クレーター周辺に飛び散っていた岩石や砂のサンプルが収集された。はやぶさ2がリュウグウの軌道を離脱し、サンプルを搬送するカプセルを地球に帰還させる軌道に入ったのが11月。カプセルが豪州南部の砂漠にパラシュートで着地したのが翌2020年12月であった。本ニュースが報じている5.4グラムのサンプルはリュウグウの地表と地表下から採集されたものだが、「20種以上のアミノ酸」は後者から検出された。5.4グラムのサンプルは国内外の8つの研究チームが分析中だが、上記のアミノ酸の検出は内2チームによるもの。アミノ酸は生物の体を作るのに欠かせないので、「生命の材料が宇宙から運ばれて生命の起源になった」という説を後押しすると注目されている。他チームの研究結果が待たれる。

(Notes)

◆ **amino acid**　アミノ酸（タンパク質を構成する有機化合物）
◆ **asteroid**　小惑星（太陽系には8つの惑星以外に無数の小さな天体がある。これらの小天体の内、周囲に円盤状に集まったガスや塵のないものを小惑星と呼ぶ。小惑星は、火星と木星の公転軌道の間に存在する小惑星帯の公転軌道上に多く賦存する）
◆ **Hayabusa2**　［宇宙航空研究開発機構（JAXA）が開発した小惑星探査機］
◆ (L. 2)　**space probe**　宇宙探査機
◆ (L. 3)　**organic compounds**　有機化合物
☞◆ (L. 5)　**hold clues to ～**　～の手掛かりとなる、糸口となる（hold/have/provide a clue to/about/as to といった動詞や前置詞も通常使われる）
◆ (L. 5-6)　**the education ministry**　文部科学省（英文正式名：Ministry of Education, Culture, Sports, Science and Technology）
◆ (L. 7)　**capsule**　カプセル（小惑星で採集したサンプルを封入したコンテナを内部に搭載。はやぶさ2の本体から切り離されたカプセルは秒速12キロで地球大気圏に再突入し、地上で回収された）
◆ (L. 8)　**surface and subsurface materials**　地表と地表下物質（から構成される試料）
◆ (L. 9)　**Ryugu asteroid**　小惑星リュウグウ（JAXAの小惑星探査プロジェクト「はやぶさ2」の目標天体。「浦島太郎」が竜宮城から玉手箱を持ち帰ることとはやぶさ2が小惑星からサンプルを持ち帰ることを掛け合わせてJAXAが命名した）
◆ (L. 9)　**300 million kilometers away**　（リュウグウは地球と同じく太陽の周りを公転しているので、軌道上の位置関係によって両者間の距離は変化する。最長で約3億6千万キロ、最も接近した場合には1千万キロ以下となる）
☞◆ (L. 10)　**unraveling the mysteries of ～**　～に関わる謎を解明する（unravelに代えて、solve, clear upなども使われる）
◆ (L. 11-12)　**presence of water and organic matter**　水と有機物の存在（「水」が存在したというのは、試料に水や氷が含まれていたわけではなく、水の成分である水素と酸素が結合した粘土鉱物が含まれていたことを指す。全体の重量の7%を水の成分が占めていることより、豊富な水が存在したとされる。その後、この天体は壊れ、一部の破片からリュウグウができたと考えられている）
◆ (L.13-14)　**Japan Aerospace Exploration Agency**　宇宙航空研究開発機構（略称：JAXA）（日本の航空宇宙開発政策を担う国立研究開発法人。本部：東京都調布市）
◆ (L. 14-15)　**The University of Tokyo**　東京大学
◆ (L. 15)　**Hiroshima University**　広島大学
◆ (L. 16)　**meteorite**　隕石
◆ (L. 17)　**meteor**　流星
◆ (L. 21)　**weathered by sunlight or cosmic rays**　太陽光や宇宙線で風化された
◆ (L. 23)　**Kensei Kobayashi**　小林憲正（横浜国立大学名誉教授、専門分野：宇宙生物学）
◆ (L. 25)　**extraterrestrial body**　地球外の天体
☞◆ (L.26)　**increases the likelihood that ～**　～という可能性を高める（文意に応じて、reduce, minimize, raiseなどの動詞も使われる）
◆ (L. 27)　**the compounds**　［ここでは「有機化合物」（organic compounds）であるamino acids（アミノ酸）を指す］
◆ (L. 28)　**natural satellite**　衛星、自然衛星、天然衛星（惑星、準惑星、小惑星の周りを公転する天体）
◆ (L. 30)　**stationary position**　定位置（リュウグウの上空20キロメートルの位置）
◆ (L. 31)　**elliptical orbit**　楕円軌道

1. 本文の内容と一致するものには T (True) を、一致しないものには F (False) を記せ。

(　　　) (1) It was in late 2020 when multiple types of amino acids were found in asteroid samples brought to Earth by the Hayabusa2 space probe.

(　　　) (2) The exploration of Ryugu was designed to find out whether sufficient amounts of amino acids and water are available for human beings to live there for any extended period.

(　　　) (3) Although one theory claimed that meteorites brought amino acids to Earth in ancient times, there was not any concluding evidence that supports this theory until Hayabusa2.

(　　　) (4) The groundbreaking achievement of Hayabusa2 was both the collection of untainted subsurface materials and sending them to the earth sealed from the atmosphere.

(　　　) (5) It took six years for more than 5.4 grams of asteroid samples to be delivered to the earth after the Hayabusa2 space probe collected them on Ryugu.

2. 本文中に掲げた［*Useful Expressions*］を参照し、下記の語群を並び替えて空欄に適語を記し、日本語に合う英文を完成させよ。

(1) 科学者達は、新型コロナウイルスが女性よりも男性の場合に悪化する傾向があるのかを理解するデータを探している。

Scientists are looking for (　　　　) (　　　　) (　　　　) (　　　　) (　　　　) why Covid-19 tends to be more severe in men than in women.

> clues　　　data　　　provide　　　that　　　to

(2) 著者は、男がどのようにしてゼロから巨万の富を築くことに成功したのか、その謎を解こうと試みた。

The author (　　　) (　　　) (　　　) (　　　) (　　　) (　　　) (　　　) the man succeeded in building his enormous wealth from scratch.

> of　　　how　　　mystery　　　solve　　　the　　　to　　　tried

(3) 現下の政局が行き詰まる中、野党二党が連立政権を組む可能性が高まっている。

The current (　　　) (　　　) (　　　) (　　　) (　　　) (　　　) that the two opposition parties will form a coalition government.

> boosted　　　deadlock　　　has　　　likelihood　　　political　　　the

音声を聞き、下線部を補え。（２回録音されています。１回目はナチュラルスピード、２回目はスロースピードです。）

Natural 33
Slow 35

Astronomers on Thursday ⁽¹⁾ _____ of the supermassive black hole at the center of the Milky Way galaxy—some 27,000 light years away from Earth. The otherworldly image of the black hole—Sagittarius A*—is just the second such photo to ever be produced, coming three years after the international Event Horizon Telescope collaboration unveiled the first view of a black hole at the center of a far-distant galaxy.

"We were stunned by how well the size of the ring agreed with predictions from Einstein's Theory of General Relativity," EHT scientist Geoffrey Bower said in a statement announcing the historic view of the gentle giant ⁽²⁾ _____ .

The "unprecedented" look at the center of the Milky Way galaxy, which contains at least 100 billion stars, has greatly improved astronomers' understanding of ⁽³⁾ _____ , Bower said.

Natural 34
Slow 36

Since Sagittarius A*—pronounced "A star"—is roughly 27,000 light-years from Earth, the black hole appears to have the same size in the sky as a donut on the moon, Event Horizon Telescope officials said in a statement Thursday announcing the discovery.

⁽⁴⁾ _____ released Thursday, astronomers in 2012 created the Event Horizon Telescope system, a global network linking eight radio observatories across the world to create a single "Earth-sized" virtual telescope.

Feryal Özel—an astronomer at the University of Arizona, where ⁽⁵⁾ _____ capturing the new image—attended a National Science Foundation press conference in Washington to announce the discovery. She described it as the "first direct image of the gentle giant" in the center of the Milky Way galaxy.

— Based on a report on nypost.com on May 12, 2022 —

〈ニュース解説〉「ブラックホール」は、太陽の数倍〜数十億倍の質量を持つ天体といわれる。恒星は水素などの燃料を燃やして輝き続けるが最後には燃え尽きる。例えていえば、風船から空気が抜けたようにぺしゃんこになり、地球がビー玉ほどに収縮した超高質量のブラックホールとなる。その存在は、物理学者アルベルト・アインシュタインが1900年代初頭に発表した「一般相対性理論」で予測したが、重力が極めて強く、光でさえものみ込まれて外に出られないため、直接観測することが困難であった。こうした中、2019年に日米欧などの国際共同研究チームが地球から約5500万光年離れた銀河「Ｍ87」の中心にある巨大ブラックホールの撮影に初めて成功した。太陽の約65億倍の質量と試算され、周囲を取り巻く光の輪の大きさは約1000億キロで太陽系がすっぽり入る規模とされる。そして、本ニュースが報じるように、2022年に同チームは太陽系を含む天の川銀河（銀河系）の中心にあるブラックホールの存在も確認した。ブラックホールはほとんどの銀河の中心部に存在し、銀河の誕生や成長と密接に関係するとみられている。具体的な役割の解明に向けた今後の研究が期待されている。

(Notes)
supermassive 超大質量　**black hole** ブラックホール　**Milky Way galaxy** 天の川銀河（銀河系）　**light years** 光年（光が１年間に真空中を進む距離。約9.5兆キロ）　**otherworldly image** 別世界の印象を与える　**Sagittarius A*** 射手座Ａスター　**international Event Horizon Telescope collaboration** 国際プロジェクト「イベント・ホライズン望遠鏡（EHT）」　**the ring**（ブラックホールを取り巻くオレンジ色のドーナツ構造の）リング　**Einstein's Theory of General Relativity** アインシュタインの一般相対性理論　**Geoffrey Bower** ジェフリー・バウワー　**gentle giant** 「優しい巨人」（射手座Ａスターにはあらゆる物質を飲み込むような活動は、現時点では見られないとして「優しい巨人」と形容されている）　**radio observatories** 宇宙電波観測所　**Feryal Özel** フェリアル・オゼール・米アリゾナ大学教授　**National Science Foundation** 米国立科学財団

■問A　空所 (a) ～ (f) にそれぞれ入るべき 1 語を下記の語群から選びその番号を記せ。

iPS（人工多能性幹）細胞	→	induced pluripotent (a) cell
タッチパネル	→	touch (b)
最先端の技術	→	(c)-of-the-art technology
高速増殖炉	→	fast breeder (d)
介護施設	→	nursing-(e) facility
生活習慣病	→	lifestyle-(f) disease

1. care	2. reactor	3. related
4. screen	5. state	6. stem

■問B　空所 (a) ～ (f) にそれぞれ入るべき 1 語を下記の語群から選びその番号を記せ。

遺伝子組み換え作物	→	genetically (a) crop
太陽光発電	→	(b) power generation
地上波デジタル放送	→	digital (c) broadcasting
医療過誤	→	medical (d)
平均寿命	→	average life (e)
介助犬	→	(f) dog

1. error	2. expectancy	3. modified
4. service	5. solar	6. terrestrial

■問C　(a) ～ (h) をそれぞれ和訳せよ。

(a) biodegradable plastic

(b) room-temperature superconductivity

(c) shape-memory garments

(d) capsule endoscope

(e) optical fiber

(f) heat stroke

(g) organ transplant

(h) brain death

Long, long, long wordy sentences ― 長い、長い、長い冗漫な文体

小説や論説等でも長くて冗長な文章は敬遠される今日である。ましてや事件や出来事の報道を行うハード・ニュースの記事は正確で簡潔（precise and concise）が生命線。即時報道を目的としないフィーチャー・ニュース、即ち特集記事や読み物においてさえも、長くて取り留めのない文体はニュース記事では避けるべきである。一昔前までは英文で論理を展開する上では理想的な句や節と考えられていた表現方法、或いは過度な丁寧表現のように相手の立場に配慮した言い回しは、ストレートさが欠ける点で逆に文章内容をより複雑にして今日の読者に分かりにくくしている場合もある。ニュース英語のみならずビジネス英語でも同じような状況に遭遇するが、文章は説明口調ではなく簡潔さを保つことによってかえって伝える側の意図が迅速に且つ正確に読者に伝わることはしばしば指摘される。下の英文は、冗漫な文の典型例であるが、冗長な文体を避けるという本課の主旨からすると真逆の書き方でそのような文体を戒めているところが面白い。文章が lengthy 或いは wordy であるということは、退屈な（tedious）文章であることと表裏一体であることを忘れるべきではない。下の英文でも分かるように、文を長くするには様々な表現や方法があるが、文を短く正確に書くことは比較的難しい。

このトピックを英文で読んでみよう。

It should be pointed out that many writers, in order to make themselves sound much more profound and scholarly than perhaps they actually are, use flabby, inflated wording such as "it should be pointed out" and "in order to" and "perhaps"—which we just did ourselves, in fact, earlier in this sentence—in addition to piling up clauses (some using dashes such as those a few words back) or parentheses, such as those in the line above, not to mention semicolons, which often suggest that the writer wants to end the sentence but just cannot bring himself to actually type a period; nonetheless, today's busy readers are too impatient to tolerate the sort of 18th-century pomposity wherein writers, so in love with the sound of their own voices, just go on and on and on and on...

NEWS MEDIA IN THE WORLD

放送 Broadcasting (1)

✓ 20世紀初頭のラジオ、その後のテレビの発達を受け、放送ニュースは即時性と広域性を武器に成長。国際ニュース放送の老舗は英国BBC（British Broadcasting Corporation）。世界中に広がる取材網を駆使、ラジオの World Service やテレビの BBC World で他をリードしてきた。米国 VOA（Voice of America）は米国国務省の対外宣伝部門として発足。冷戦時代には東側への西側意見の伝達役を担ったが、現在は、世界的なニュース専門機関の地位を確立している。

NEWS 14

Disk 2
Underdogs no more: Japan looks toward 2023 Rugby World Cup

WELLINGTON, New Zealand—Michael Leitch led Japan to key victories at the last two rugby World Cups. The next World Cup is in 2023 in France, and Leitch has a message: Don't overlook Japan.

In 2015, Japan defeated South Africa in the English seaside town of Brighton, which lives on as the "Brighton Miracle." In 2019, its group-stage wins over Ireland 5 and Scotland carried it to the quarterfinals and brought rugby into the daylight in Japan.

Leitch is no longer the captain but is still a player and a key member of the team. He looks forward to the tournament where Japan is drawn in group D with England, Argentina, Samoa and one other qualifier. 10

The underdog tag doesn't rankle Leitch—nor does he see it as appropriate. Leitch told reporters this week, "We still are regarded as an underdog despite having had two successful World Cup campaigns. It's a hard one to brush off."

Leitch said it's difficult to judge where Japan stands in its World Cup preparation compared to the build-up to the 2019. Then, as Japan prepared to host the world 15 tournament at home for the first time, a sense of urgency and purpose powered the campaign.

The years since haven't worked to Japan's advantage in the same way. Covid-19 shut international borders and Japan went 18 months without a test match. Its ability to introduce new players was impaired, but Leitch believes things are now on course. 20 "This time around it's a bit different with Covid," he added. "It's really hard to gauge where we are with our preparation, but with the time we have been together, we've made incredible progress."

Leitch said Japan can be confident in the players it likely will take to the World Cup. Many already have World Cup experience, while younger players have had 25 the opportunity to play beside or against some of the world's top players in Japan's rapidly improving professional league.

"I'd say we've got quite a good core of players that have been involved in both 2015 and 2019 World Cup, the majority in 2019," Leitch said. "I think that knowledge and experience that we have is going to be crucial in 2023." "We've got 30 some great up-and-coming players who have got real X-factor," he added.

Japan's image is that it relies on speed rather than physicality, but Leitch said that is changing.

— Based on a report in Mainichi.com on May 4, 2022 —

〈ニュース解説〉　ラグビー・ワールドカップ 2015 年大会（イングランド開催。一部の試合はウェールズのカーディフ開催）と日本で開催された 2019 年大会において、予想を上回る活躍で注目を集めた日本代表は、2023 年フランス大会に向けて準備を進めている。国内リーグでは、2021 年 6 月に、これまで 18 年続いたトップリーグに代わってリーグワンが発足し、海外からの有力選手も加わり日本代表の強化にも貢献している。一方、フランス大会を前に、コロナ禍で外国の代表チームとのテストマッチの数が少なくなる中、現在のチーム状態を把握する上で不安が残るが、過去 2 大会の経験や若手の台頭等の明るい材料もある。Brave Blossoms は日本代表の愛称。

(Notes)　【※☞マークは *Useful Expressions*】

◆　**2023 Rugby World Cup**　2023 年にフランスで開催されるラグビー・ワールドカップ

◆　(L. 1)　**Michael Leitch**　マイケル・リーチ（ニュージーランド出身のラグビー選手。2013 年に日本に帰化した後、2014 年から 21 年まで日本代表キャプテンをつとめる）

◆　(L. 5)　**Brighton Miracle**　（2015 年イングランド大会において、日本代表が初戦で優勝候補の南アフリカ代表を撃破した試合を、開催地ブライトンの名を取って「ブライトンの奇跡」と称する）

◆　(L. 5)　**group-stage**　グループリーグの［日本語では通常グループリーグと称される。全チームを数組に分け、決勝トーナメント（knockout stage）に進む前に各組で行われる総あたりのリーグ戦。通常最上位チームか上位 2 チームが決勝トーナメントに進む］

◆　(L. 10)　**one other qualifier**　もう一つの予選通過チーム（この記事が書かれた段階では決まっていなかったが、その後南米のチリがこのグループ D に加わることになった）

◆　(L. 11)　**underdog tag**　負け犬のレッテル（長い間ラグビー・ワールドカップで成績が低迷した日本代表に付けられた一方的・断定的な評価。1995 年の南アフリカ大会で、ニュージーランド代表を相手に 145 対 17 の記録的大差で惨敗したことも悪印象となった。直近 2 大会での大活躍にもかかわらず、一度貼られたレッテルを剥がすのはむずかしい）

◆　(L. 15)　**build-up to the 2019**　2019 年日本大会に向けての強化（自国開催でもあり、特別な強化策が策定された）

☞◆　(L. 20-21)　**Leitch believes things are now on course**　リーチは、現在の状況は順調であると考えている（things は、物事を特定せずにやや曖昧に物事、状況、事情を漠然と表すので詳説する手間が省け、英語ニュースの会話部分を含め会話で頻繁に使用される。be on course は順調に、予定通りの方向に進んで、の意。）

◆　(L. 26-27)　**Japan's rapidly improving professional league**　急速にレベルアップしつつある日本のプロリーグ（2021 年発足したリーグワンの事に言及しているが、リーグワンは完全プロ化構想であるが、まだ実現していない。現在も企業に属し正社員としてラグビーをする選手が多い）

☞◆　(L. 31)　**up-and-coming**　前途有望な、新進気鋭の

◆　(L. 31)　**X-factor**　未知の要因、能力

◆　(L. 32)　**physicality**　肉体的力、フィジカル

1. 本文の内容と一致するものには T (True) を、一致しないものには F (False) を記せ。

(   ) (1) Michael Leitch's confidence in the Japanese rugby team waned after its dismal performance during the 2019 Rugby World Cup.

(   ) (2) Japan recorded wins over South Africa, Ireland and Scotland all at the same World Cup.

(   ) (3) Leitch seems to accept the low rating of the Japanese rugby team.

(   ) (4) It can reasonably be surmised that Japan's preparation efforts for the next World Cup are much less than satisfactory.

(   ) (5) The article seems to assume that the participation of foreign players in the Japanese rugby league has left a positive impact on the sport.

(   ) (6) With the declining physical strength of its experienced players, Japanese rugby needs to nurture young talent.

2. 本文中に掲げた下記の［*Useful Expressions*］を用いて空欄に適語を記し、日本語に合う英文を完成させよ。

(1) 〈**things**〉

(   ) where women's status is much lower than men's.

女性の地位が男性よりずっと低いこの国では状況は違っている。

(2) 〈**be on course**〉

Despite Covid-19 restrictions, (   ) for recovery.

コロナ禍の制限にも関わらず、ホテル業界は今や回復基調に戻りつつある。

(3) 〈**up-and-coming**〉

She is (   ) MPs of the Conservative Party.

彼女は保守党の新進気鋭の女性議員の一人である。（MP は member of parliament の略語。英国等で下院議員を指す）

音声を聞き、下線部を補え。（２回録音されています。１回目はナチュラルスピード、２回目はスロースピードです。）

   Japanese all-time great figure skater Yuzuru Hanyu announced his retirement from competition on Tuesday, marking the end of a stellar career that included breaking more than a dozen world records and winning two Olympic gold medals. The 27-year-old, dressed in a suit and tie at a news conference in Tokyo, said that, while he was stepping back from competition, he would 5
(1) _____.

   He added he would keep striving to achieve the fabled quadruple axel—which has never been completed in competition—(2) _____ at the 2022 Beijing Winter Olympics.

   Hanyu, a two-time world champion and winner of four Grand Prix Finals, 10
(3) _____—including a massive following in China—as the "Ice Prince."

   Hanyu expressed his "deepest gratitude" to his fans on Tuesday, adding he hoped people would continue supporting him. Many fans flooded to social media
(4) _____ on Tuesday, thanking him for his hard work and 15 dedication to the sport over the years.

   Hanyu won his first gold medal at the Sochi 2014 Winter Olympics at age 19, becoming the youngest men's champion since 1948 and (5) _____
_____ figure skating gold. His Sochi performance made him an immediate star and arguably Japan's most famous athlete. 20

— *Based on a report on CNN.com on July 19, 2022* —

〈ニュース解説〉　日本を代表するフィギュアスケーター羽生結弦選手が引退を表明。今後はプロのアスリートとしてスケートを続けていくとのことで、引退というより新たな一歩のスタートと表現した方がよさそうである。中国を含め世界中に多くのファンを持つ羽生。自身とファンの双方から感謝の気持ちが伝えられ、引退は冷静に受け止められている。

(Notes)

quadruple axel 4 回転アクセル、4 回転半ジャンプ（quad axel とも呼ばれる。後ろ向きに跳ぶトゥループ、サルコウ、ルッツと違い、アクセルは前向きに跳んで着氷は後ろ向きとなるため、4 回転半を跳ぶことになり難易度が高い。羽生の 4 回転アクセルは、史上初めて認定されたが回転不足と判定された）　**2022 Beijing Winter Olympics** 2022 年北京冬季オリンピック大会（2022 年 2 月に 17 日間にわたって北京市及び隣接する河北省張家口市で開催された中国初の冬季オリンピック。新型コロナウイルスの感染拡大を受け、チケットは外国人へはもちろんのこと一般販売はされず、観客を限定して受け入れた）　**Grand Prix Final** グランプリ・ファイナル［フィギュアスケートのグランプリシリーズの 6 つの大会（米、加、中、仏、露、日で開催）での成績上位者が出場し、その年のナンバーワンを決する決勝大会。過去に羽生結弦が 4 連覇、女子では浅田真央が 4 回優勝を飾っている］　**Sochi 2014 Winter Olympics** 2014 年ソチ冬季オリンピック（黒海に面したロシア最大の保養地ソチで開催された）

■問A　相撲で用いられる次の用語に対する英語表現を下記の語群から選びその番号を記せ。

(a) 寄り切り　　　　(b) つり出し　　　　(c) 上手投げ

(d) 下手投げ　　　　(e) まげ　　　　　　(f) 親方

(g) 押し出し　　　　(h) 土俵入り　　　　(i) 横綱

1. forcing out	2. grand champion	3. lifting out
4. overarm throw	5. pushing out	6. ring entering ceremony
7. stable master	8. topknot	9. underarm throw

■問B　(a) ～ (g) の体操用語にそれぞれ対応する日本語表現を下記の語群から選びその番号を記せ。

(a) balance beam　　(b) floor exercise　　(c) flying rings　　(d) horse vault

(e) parallel bars　　(f) pommel horse　　(g) uneven bars

1. あん馬	2. 段違い平行棒	3. 跳馬	4. つり輪
5. 平均台	6. 平行棒	7. ゆか	

■問C　(a) ～ (f) のラグビー用語の英文の説明に対応する英語を下記の語群から選びその番号を記せ。

(a) The eight forwards from each team binding together and pushing against each other

(b) The area where a player must remain for a minimum of 10 minutes after being shown a yellow card

(c) An offence whereby a player deliberately impedes an opponent who does not have the ball

(d) A charge executed on a player who has already passed or kicked away the ball

(e) A physical contact that is formed, usually following a tackle, when the ball is on the ground and players from two opposing teams meet over the ball

(f) The player who usually wears jersey number 15 and acts as the last line of defence

1. fullback　2. late tackle　3. obstruction　4. ruck　5. scrum　6. sin bin

Jargon and journalese — 専門用語とジャーナリズム調の文体

ニュースにとって最も重要なことは「分かりやすい」ことだ。誰もが忙しい現代、基本的に「読み捨て」される新聞記事は誰が読んでもきちんと内容が伝わること、いちいち読み返さなくても分かることが非常に重要だからである。英語の新聞の場合でも、難解な言葉や表現を避け、単語そのものもできるだけわかりやすい short words を用いる。例えば purchase → buy、attempt → try、anticipate → expect、utilize → use、request → ask、obtain → get などである。しかし、時に新聞記事は陳腐で大げさなジャーナリズム的表現に陥りがちであることも事実だ。

このトピックを英文で読んでみよう。

Bureaucrats love to use words like *utilize*, *finalize*, and *structured*. Cops like to say suspects are *apprehended* and *incarcerated*. And if you are a campus spokesman, why would you want to say "*the school can't afford to pay raises*" when you could say "*the salary scale revision will adversely affect the university's financial stability*"?

Good reporters relentlessly strive to filter out bloated, convoluted jargon and officialese. And those who do not should be *redirected*, *transitioned*, or *subject to personnel surplus reduction* (i.e., fired).

But reporters often lapse into "journalese" without realizing it. Journalese, as veteran editor Joe Grimm puts it, is the peculiar language that newspapers have evolved that reads like this:

Negotiators yesterday, in an eleventh-hour decision following marathon talks, hammered out an agreement on a key wage provision they earlier had rejected.

That's not as bad as bureaucratic gobbledygook. But it is still a problem, because it is still full of clichés.

放送 Broadcasting (2)

✓ 放送産業の故郷米国では、ラジオ放送についで、1940 年代には商業テレビ放送が開始。CBS（Columbia Broadcasting System）、NBC（National Broadcasting Company）、ABC（American Broadcasting Company）の 3 大ネットワーク時代が続いたが、現在では FOX を含め 4 大ネットワークと呼ばれることもある。さらに地上波放送に飽き足らない視聴者のニーズに応える形でケーブルテレビが急拡大。80 年代には CNN（Cable News Network）が衛星放送による世界初のニュース専門テレビ局として誕生。衛星放送が東側住民へ情報を提供し、冷戦終結に貢献したという評価もある。

NEWS 15

Disk 2

World Athletics president calls future of women's sport 'fragile,' defends testosterone regulations

The president of World Athletics, Sebastian Coe, reportedly said that the integrity and future of women's sport is "fragile" and defended his governing body's rules on testosterone, according to the Times of London. His comments came days after American swimmer Lia Thomas became the first transgender woman to win an NCAA swimming championship last week.　5

University of Pennsylvania swimmer Thomas last week became the first out transgender athlete to win an NCAA Division I title after finishing first in the women's 500-yard freestyle event. Thomas, who previously swam for the men's team at UPenn, has been the target of intense scrutiny in the US as many states have moved to limit the participation of transgender women in women's sports.　10

Her success has sparked questions, especially in right-wing media and among Republican politicians, about what makes for fair competition and who gets to be counted as a woman. According to World Athletics rules, which govern track and field events—and do not apply to swimming—a transgender woman must demonstrate that she has had testosterone levels continuously below 5 nmol per liter　15 for a period of at least 12 months to be allowed to compete and must keep those levels "for so long as she wishes to maintain her eligibility to compete in the female category of competition."

"There is no question to me that testosterone is the key determinant in performance," Coe said. But a 2017 study in the journal Sports Medicine found "no　20 direct or consistent research" of trans people having an athletic advantage over their cisgender peers. There is debate in the scientific community as to whether androgenic hormones like testosterone are useful markers of athletic advantage.

For over a decade, the NCAA has required transgender women to be on testosterone suppression treatment for a year before they are allowed to compete　25 on a women's team. But in January, the NCAA said it would take a sport-by-sport approach to its rules on transgender athletes' participation and defer to each sport's national governing body.

USA Swimming then released a set of stricter guidelines that require elite trans women athletes to have at least three continuous years of testosterone levels below　30 5 nmol per liter and to prove to a panel of medical experts that they do not have a competitive advantage over cisgender women.

—Based on a report on CNN.com on March 22, 2022 —

〈ニュース解説〉　全米大学スポーツ協会（NCAA）の水泳競技で、トランスジェンダー（transgender）の女性競泳選手が優勝しその公平性について一部から異議が唱えられた。世界のスポーツ界では、男性から女性への性別適合手術やホルモン療法後の身体能力のシスジェンダー（cisgender）選手に対する優位性とジェンダー平等に関連した議論が絶えない。イングランドの女子ラグビーでは、トランスジェンダー選手の女子ラグビーの試合への出場が安全面を考慮して禁止されている。一般的には、トランスジェンダー選手が男性ホルモンであるテストステロン値を抑えられるかどうかが競技の公平性を保てるかどうかの判断基準であるが、性の多様性（gender diversity）が叫ばれる昨今、男と女という性別二元論（gender binary）の議論だけで十分なのかとの指摘もあり、議論が複雑化している。

(Notes)　【※☞マークは *Useful Expressions*】

◆ **World Athletics**　ワールドアスレティックス［各国の陸上競技加盟団体を統括し、世界的陸上競技大会の運営を担う国際競技連盟。旧称の「国際陸上競技連盟（IAAF）」に代わって、2019 年 11 月から用いられている名称。日本陸上競技連盟では、日本語表記は「ワールドアスレティックス」、日本語呼称は「世界陸連」を使用］

◆ (L. 1)　**Sebastian Coe**　セバスティアン・コー（ワールドアスレティックスの現会長。2015 年から会長職にある。陸上競技中距離種目の世界的ランナーで、モスクワ、ロサンジェルス五輪の 1500m で連続金メダルを獲得）

☞◆ (L. 1)　**reportedly**　報道によれば、伝えられるところによれば［allegedly 同様、筆者（記者）が断定を避けて表現したい場合等、ニュースの初期段階の報道でしばしば用いられる］

◆ (L. 2)　**his governing body**　コーが会長を務めるワールドアスレティックスを指す

◆ (L. 3)　**testosterone**　テストステロン（男性の主要な性ホルモンであり、男性生殖組織の発達に加え、筋肉や骨等の増加・成長にも重要な役割を果たす。逆に、テストステロンが抑制されると、筋肉や骨の成長が抑えられる）

◆ (L. 3)　**the Times of London**　英国の日刊紙タイムズ（The Times）［ニューヨークタイムズ等と区別するため、The Times of London 或いは The London Times と呼ばれることもある。メディア王ルパート・マードック率いるニューズ・コープ（News Corp）の傘下にある］

◆ (L. 5)　**NCAA**　全米大学体育協会（National Collegiate Athletic Association の略称。米国の大学スポーツの統括協会であり、様々な大学スポーツ競技の運営支援等も行う）

◆ (L. 6)　**University of Pennsylvania**　ペンシルヴァニア大学（フィラデルフィア所在の私立大学。米国の名門私大連合であるアイビー・リーグの一校で、最難関大学の一つである。後述の UPenn と略されることもある）

◆ (L. 7)　**transgender**　トランスジェンダー［出生届等に記載された性別と自身の性同一性（gender identity）やジェンダー表現とが異なる場合や異なる人を指す。則ち、身体的性別と性自認が一致しない人］

◆ (L. 15)　**nmol per liter**　ナノモル毎リットル（nanomoles per liter のことで、質量測定に使われる。ナノモルは 10 億分の 1 モル。liter は米国綴りで英国等では litre が一般的）

◆ (L. 20)　**Sports Medicine**　スポーツ・メディスン誌（シュプリンガー・ネイチャー社発行の雑誌。当該論文は、2017 年 4 月発行の同誌 47 巻、4 号に掲載されている）

◆ (L. 22)　**cisgender**　シスジェンダー（出生時の身体的性別と性自認が同一の人。"cis-" はフランス語由来で、"trans-" の対義接頭辞）

◆ (L. 22)　**androgenic**　男性的特徴を生じる

☞◆ (L. 29)　**a set of**　一連の（a series of や an array of も似たような表現である）

1. 本文の内容と一致するものには T (True) を、一致しないものには F (False) を記せ。

(　　) (1) World Athletics president Sebastian Coe was rather reluctant to express his opinion regarding transgender athletes' participation in women's sports.

(　　) (2) The controversy over Lia Thomas was not handled appropriately by the NCAA, causing World Athletics president to step in to the debate.

(　　) (3) Lia Thomas's win appears to be becoming a political issue involving party politicians.

(　　) (4) World Athletics rules expect a transgender athlete to continuously suppress the level of testosterone below 5 nmol per liter mark.

(　　) (5) Everyone agrees that transgender athletes have obvious advantage over their cisgender counterparts.

(　　) (6) Most scientists opine that androgenic hormones like testosterone can work as good indicators of trans women's physical advantage in athletics.

(　　) (7) The NCAA tries to supervise all the collegiate sports closely in terms of transgender athletes' issues.

2. 本文中に掲げた下記の [*Useful Expressions*] を用いて空欄に適語を記し、日本語に合う英文を完成させよ。

(1) ⟨**reportedly**⟩

His wife is (　　　　　　　　　　　　　　　　).

伝えられるところでは、彼の妻は癌を患っている。

(2) ⟨**a set of**⟩

In the interview, you are expected (　　　　　　　　　　　) about your college life.

面接では、あなたの大学生活についての一連の質問に答えていただくことになります。

音声を聞き、下線部を補え。（2回録音されています。1回目はナチュラルスピードです。）

Natural
45

Slow
47

Just a week after he threw Japanese baseball's first perfect game in 28 years, pitching sensation Roki Sasaki [(1)] _____. On April 10, the 20-year-old Chiba Lotte Marines pitcher struck out 19 batters, tying the Nippon Professional Baseball (NPB) record, in an all-time great performance against the Orix Buffaloes. During that stretch, Sasaki [(2)] _____ _____, setting a new NPB record.

5

Then, on Sunday, the wunderkind threw eight more perfect innings against the Hokkaido Nippon Ham Fighters to strike out 14 batters, before being pulled by the Marines [(3)] _____. The Marines went on to lose 1-0 in 10 innings against the Ham Fighters.

10

Natural
46

Slow
48

Despite the loss, Sasaki has now thrown a remarkable 17 consecutive perfect innings and [(4)] _____, a new NPB record. "He [Sasaki] is just too tough," Ham Fighters' game-winner Chusei Mannami told the Japan Times. "The way that forkball drops? Forget about it."

Remember the name because it wouldn't be beyond Sasaki to throw another perfect game this season—or [(5)] _____ the MLB sometime in the near future.

15

— Based on a report on CNN.com on April 18, 2022 —

〈ニュース解説〉「令和の怪物」とも称される千葉ロッテマリーンズ所属の佐々木朗希投手は、2022年4月10日に行われたオリックス・バッファロー戦で登板し、日本新記録となる13者連続奪三振を記録、さらに28年ぶり史上16人目となる完全試合を達成した。日本プロ野球史上最年少での完全試合達成であった。その1週間後の4月17日の北海道日本ハムファイターズ戦では、佐々木は8回まで投げて打者を一人も出さなかった。

(Notes)
perfect game 完全試合（エラー、四球、死球があっても達成できるノーヒットノーランとは違い、先発投手が相手チームの打者を一度も出塁させずに勝利すること）　**Chiba Lotte Marines** 千葉ロッテマリーンズ（日本プロ野球パシフィック・リーグ所属。本拠地は千葉市美浜区のZOZOマリンスタジアム）　**Nippon Professional Baseball** 日本野球機構（日本プロ野球を統括する一般社団法人）　**Orix Buffaloes** オリックス・バファローズ（パシフィック・リーグ所属の日本プロ野球球団。本拠地は大阪市の京セラドーム）　**wunderkind** 神童（ドイツ語のヴンダーキントから。英語のprodigyに相当）　**Hokkaido Nippon Ham Fighters** 北海道日本ハムファイターズ（パシフィック・リーグ所属の日本プロ野球球団。2023年シーズンより、本拠地を札幌ドームから北広島市のドーム球場「エスコン・フィールド北海道」に移す予定）　**game-winner Chusei Mannami** 決勝点をたたき出した万波中正。万波は日本ハムファイターズの外野手　**forkball** フォークボール。投手の投げたボールが打者近くで急に落下する変化球。人差し指と中指でボールを挟んで投げる。米国ではスプリッター（splitter）と呼ばれるが、日本でもボールの挟み方を浅くして急速を上げたフォークボールをスプリットと呼ぶことがある　**MLB** メジャーリーグ（Major League Baseballの略）

■問A (a) ～ (i) にそれぞれ対応する英語表現を下記の語群から選びその番号を記せ。

(a) 円盤投げ	(b) 砲丸投げ	(c) やり投げ
(d) ハンマー投げ	(e) 走高跳び	(f) 走幅跳び
(g) 三段跳び	(h) 棒高跳び	(i) 十種競技

1. decathlon	2. discus throw	3. hammer throw
4. high jump	5. javelin throw	6. long jump
7. pole vault	8. shot put	9. triple jump

■問B (a) ～ (h) の野球用語の説明に対応する英語を下記の語群から選びその番号を記せ。

(a) The extension of a baseball game until one team is ahead of the other at the end of an inning

(b) An out resulting from a batter getting three strikes during a time at bat

(c) Getting two players out on one play

(d) An act of deliberately hitting a baseball gently without swinging the bat so that it does not roll far into the infield

(e) A pitch that the catcher should have caught but missed, allowing runners to advance to the next base

(f) A relief pitcher who specializes in protecting a lead by getting the final outs in a close game

(g) A way of measuring a pitcher's effectiveness

(h) A pitch of a baseball that does not travel straight, as it is thrown with spin so that its path curves as it approaches the batter

1. breaking ball	2. bunt	3. closer	4. double play
5. earned run average	6. extra innings	7. passed ball	8. strikeout

Clichés（クリシェ）— 使い古された常套句

クリシェ（cliché）はフランス語語源で、「使い古され手垢がついてしまった陳腐な常套句」を意味する。元々は目新しくインパクトのある表現だったが、あまりにも使われすぎたため陳腐化してしまった比喩、イディオム、キャッチフレーズ、（聖書、文学作品、映画のセリフ等からの）引用、ことわざ、外来語、流行語などが含まれる。ライターの頭の中にはクリシェが定着してしまっているので、ニュースを書く際にも安易に、あるいは、無意識にクリシェを使ってしまいがちである。しかし、クリシェの使用は文を空疎で魅力のないものにしてしまう危険性があるので、できるだけ回避するのが望ましいとされている。*The New York Times Manual of Style and Usage* でも、「クリシェを用いる場合にはそれらを用いることに妥当性があるか否か（whether their use can be justified）を慎重に検討すべきだが、大抵の場合、その使用に妥当性はない」としている。クリシェと思われる表現をニュースの中で使おうとする場合には、その適切性・新鮮味をきちんと吟味することが必須である。*News Reporting and Writing*（Menche, 1987）によると、英国の作家でジャーナリストでもある George Orwell（ジョージ・オウェル）も、「印刷物で見慣れた表現を使用する時には常に慎重に」とライターに警告している。

このトピックを英文で読んでみよう。

Beyond the shadow of a doubt, you should work 24/7 to avoid clichés like the plague. Hel-*lo*? It's a no-brainer. Go ahead—make my day.

Tired, worn-out clichés instantly lower the IQ of your writing. So do corny newswriting clichés (a form of journalese) like these:

The *close-knit community* was *shaken by the tragedy*.

Tempers flared over a laundry list of complaints.

The *embattled mayor* is *cautiously optimistic*, but *troubled youths* face an *uncertain future* sparked by *massive blasts* in *bullet-riddled, shark-infested waters*.

So *now begins the heartbreaking task of cleaning up*.

Yes, clichés *can* come in handy. And yes, a skilled writer can use them in clever ways. Once in a blue moon.

NEWS MEDIA IN THE WORLD

放送 Broadcasting (3)

✓　CNN の成功を受け、90 年代以降ニュース専門チャンネルが続々登場。米国では、映像産業から派生した米国 FOX ニュースが参入。中東カタールにはアル・ジャジーラ（Al Jazeera）が誕生。インターネットとの融合による映像情報サービスの拡大を背景に、既存ニュース・メディアも含めた世界大のメディアミックス競争が進行中だ。

参考文献

R.E. Garst & T.M. Bernstein, *Headlines and Deadlines*, Columbia University Press (1963)

L.A. Campbell & R.E. Wolseley, *How to Report and Write the News*, Prentice-Hall (1961)

Tim Harrower, *Inside Reporting*, McGraw-Hill (2009)

The Missouri Group, *News Reporting and Writing*, Bedford / St Martins (2010)

William E. Blundell, *The Art and Craft of Feature Writing based on The Wall Street Journal Guide*, Plume (1988)

Darrell Christian, *The Associated Press Stylebook 2010 and Briefing on Media Law*, Associated Press (2010)

Rene J. Cappon, *The Associated Press Guide to News Writing*, 3rd ed., ARCO (2005),

Bill Kovach & Tom Rosenstiel, *The Elements of Journalism*, Three Rivers Press (2007)

Allan M. Siegal and William G. Connolly, *The New York Times Manual of Style and Usage*, Three Rivers Press (1999)

Paul R. Martin, (2002), *The Wall Street Journal Essential Guide to Business Style and Usage*, Free Press (2002)

Thomas W. Lippman, *The Washington Post Desk-Book on Style*, 2nd ed., McGraw-Hill (1989)

Brian S. Brooks & James L. Pinson, *Working with Words*, 2nd ed., St. Martin,s Press (1993)

Carole Rich, *Writing and Reporting News*, 5th ed., Thomson Wadsworth (2002)

藤井章雄, 『放送ニュース英語　音を読む』, 朝日出版社 (1983)

藤井章雄, 『ニュース英語がわかる本』, PHP 研究所 (1992)

藤井章雄, 『ニュース英語の翻訳プロセス』, 早稲田大学出版部 (1996)

藤井章雄, 『放送ニュース英語の体系』, 早稲田大学出版部 (2004)

日本英語コミュニケーション学会紀要　第 7 巻 (1998), 8 巻 (1999), 11 巻 (2002), 12 巻 (2003), 13 巻 (2004), 15 巻 (2006), 17 巻 (2008), 18 巻 (2009), 19 巻 (2010), 20 巻 (2011), 21 巻 (2012), 22 巻 (2013)

時事英語の総合演習
—2023 年度版—

検印
省略

© 2023年 1 月31日　第 1 版発行

編著者　　　　　堀江　洋文
　　　　　　　　加藤　香織
　　　　　　　　小西　和久
　　　　　　　　宮崎　修二
　　　　　　　　内野　泰子

発行者　　　　　小川　洋一郎

発行所　　　　　　　株式会社　朝 日 出 版 社
　　　　101-0065　東京都千代田区西神田 3-3-5
　　　　　　　　　電話　東京 (03)3239-0271
　　　　　　　　　FAX　東京 (03)3239-0479
　　　　　　　　e-mail　text-e@asahipress.com
　　　　　　　　振替口座　00140-2-46008
　　　　　組版／製版・信毎書籍印刷株式会社

ISBN 978-4-255-15698-9　C 1082